The Book of Change

The 7 Essential Elements to Manage Your Evolution to Success

Tony Debogorski

The Book of Change

All rights reserved. No portion of this book may be reproduced mechanically, electronically, or by any other means, including photocopying, without permission of the publisher or author except in the case of brief quotations embodied in critical articles and reviews. It is illegal to copy this book, post it to a website, or distribute it by any other means without permission from the publisher or author.

Limits of Liability and Disclaimer of Warranty
The author and publisher shall not be liable for your misuse of this material. This book is strictly for informational and educational purposes.

Warning – Disclaimer
The purpose of this book is to educate and entertain. The author and/or publisher do not guarantee that anyone following these techniques, suggestions, tips, ideas, or strategies will become successful. The author and/or publisher shall have neither liability nor responsibility to anyone with respect to any loss or damage caused, or alleged to be caused, directly or indirectly by the information contained in this book.

Publisher
10-10-10 Publishing
Markham, ON

Copyright © 2016 by Tony Debogorski
ISBN: 978-1-77277-106-0
Printed in Canada and the United States of America

Contents

Dedication	v
Foreword	vii
Acknowledgements	ix
Chapter 1: My Story	1
Chapter 2: Lessons Learned from My Three Major Failures	9
Chapter 3: Lessons Learned from My Three Major Successes	23
Chapter 4: My Newest Success	45
Chapter 5: Continuing Education	63
Chapter 6: Hopes and Dreams for the Future	75
Chapter 7: Move Forward With Me	89
Conclusion	107
About the Author	109
Testimonials	111

Dedication

*I would like to dedicate this book to all the
wonderful people I have met and influenced me to
this point in my life; my amazing family, who mean the
world to me for their encouragement and support;
and especially my son, daughter and my
most wonderful, loving and supportive wife.*

Foreword

I have known Tony Debogorski for over two decades. During that time, I have watched him weather a variety of life changing events, from divorce through business investments gone bad. Through it all, I have seen Tony demonstrate a remarkable resilience. How does he manage to not only survive, but also thrive during the adjustments that might be overwhelming for the rest of the world?

Throughout *The Book on Change,* Tony discusses tactics that he has used to weather change, but also shares his own story of what he has learned from both his failures and successes. This book gives you real life examples of how you too can thrive during times of intense upheaval in your own life. From owning your own business to personal relationships, Tony covers how you can make change work for you, instead of fearing the changes in your own life.
Tony has truly tapped into the best strategies for making times of change exciting, instead of dreading change. Are you looking for strategies to move forward after a major life event? Tony has you covered with approaches that can help you to make peace with the change in your own life, but also help you to embrace the benefits of change!

Raymond Aaron
New York Times Best Selling Author

Acknowledgements

I would like to acknowledge the many individuals I have met to date for their encouragement, support and friendship: Johnny and Wanda Halerewich, Mike and Pat Halerewich, Joe and Agnes Halerewich, Annie and Wendlin Gerk, Bob Becker, Mark Dollevoet, Mike Dollevoet, Greg Debogorski, Carmen Haas, Shawn Cameron, Doug Lovsin, Frank Lovsin, Bill Miller, Dan Payerl, Carmine Falcone, Everett George, Ernie Haas, Bill Fletcher, Morag Harmsen, Daryl Stien, Jim Clark, Mike Wood, Steve Cathcart, Jim Nicoletti, Lee Tipman, Bruce Hutton, Bernie Stoski, Mark Hoffman, Mike Gerencser, Troy Moller, Scott Bullock, Tim Stanley, Rob Allan, Alex Debogorski, Don Mercier, John Vlooswyk, Dominic Sorrentino, Mike Korcuba, Martin Wood, Ted Tobias, Kevin Johnstone, Mike Colombo, Greg and Karen Heath, Scott Grant, Dave Brown, Nick Stryland, Raymond Aaron, Mike Schryer, Ray Bernard, Brian Barnett, and Jim Haines, just to name a few. These people have all had a significant personal influence on my life. Without them, and many others unmentioned, this book would not have been possible.

Dedication in memorandum

I would like to dedicate this book to my late father, Eugene Debogorski, and my good friend, Marshall Munroe. Both of these men emphasized "loyalty" as a trait of utmost importance, and they placed high value in a handshake. I am blessed for having had them in my life. They are both missed as they left this world too soon.

Chapter 1

My Story

Meeting Raymond Aaron

I was born into and grew up in a rural farm family in northern Alberta, Canada. Our family was built on the idea of working hard and building what you had with your own two hands. I learned to be a jack of all trades in order to get things done around the farm. When I went away to get my university education, the idea was that I would receive my education, come home and get a job, marry my high school girlfriend, Carmen, and then raise my family close to home. In fact, I was one of only a few family members that received a university education. Working hard was a way of life, but the idea of working smarter, not harder, was a fairly new concept to me. Building from nothing was not new, but how I built something from nothing was just through plain sweat and hard work. I couldn't really imagine any other way.

Shortly after graduating from university, I came across an ad that struck me because it was outside my everyday routine. It was an ad offering a real estate investing course that would last one weekend long. That course introduced me to Raymond Aaron and began a 25-year friendship and partnership. He is my mentor, because he really has always talked straight. Although in 1991, he was very straightforward and to the point, almost gruff, his no nonsense approach got results. At the same time, that weekend changed the course of my life. Suddenly, I could imagine a life different from the one that had been laid out before me. Change was entering my life for the first time in a dramatic way, although I didn't realize that at the time.

I spent that first weekend absorbing the knowledge that Raymond offered, taking away the idea that I could afford to buy my first home. Considering I had just left university, was starting my new career and life, the idea of risking my little bit of savings seemed almost crazy. But I made the leap, scrapping together a $10,000 down payment for my first home. This home was now my family home, where my new wife and I set up our life as newlyweds.

My first wife was someone I had known for years. We attended university together and eventually got married. Buying that first home felt like a financial victory, despite the fact that we were still just starting out. Yet, I also had begun to increase my knowledge of real estate, allowing me to consider another means of providing for my new family beyond the typical corporate rat race.

What is important to note is change often happens first in your own mind. By opening my mind to the idea that I could make money in alternative fashions, I was taking that first step in terms of getting comfortable with change. Throughout the next few decades, I was going to encounter some major personal milestones that would prompt me to make some big changes, in my mindset and my financial circumstances. I also learned that I did not have to do it alone and that it was OK to find and utilize mentors.

Growing My Real Estate Business

My second opportunity to get a stake in the real estate game was when I joined a group (Real Estate Investment Network or REIN). For my first investment, I used credit cards to fund the initial down payments, then, after some time went by, the house was refinanced to pay back the card. Suddenly, I was a student with investments that over five years grew in value to be worth over $500,000. In the early 1990s, that was big money.

While I had at this point moved into the corporate world, the real estate business had become a side line that provided a nice source of additional income and hope for the future. I continued to look for additional real estate to invest in, but my family was fairly secure financially, so I got comfortable.
The reality is that change is happening in our lives, whether we want to admit it or not. Technology, society and even government are prompting constant change in our lives. We adapt to it, eventually coming to a point where it almost seems as if we have always had those changes in our lives. They become routine.

Here are just a few of the changes that I have personally seen in areas of technology for example. Does anyone even remember the typewriter? When I left university and started working, these were still fairly common. Today, almost everyone works with a computer, multiple programs are connected to their office through a personal computer that they can carry in their hand. Yes, I am talking about your (smart) phone.

The internet has completely changed how we interact with each other. In a matter of minutes, I can connect with individuals on six different continents.

While it seems routine today, the reality is that ability is really only a couple of decades old. But for those born before the 1990s, we all have stories of life prior to the internet. Take a moment to imagine some of the changes you personally may have seen. The reality is that change is always happening around and to us. Yet to embrace change requires more from us than just going with the flow. In fact, change is occurring around us at a pace that is greater than any other time in history. I will discuss more about that later. Right now, I am going to share with you one of the major life changes that happened to me just a few years after my marriage.

Dramatic Life Change - Divorce

In 1996, my first wife convinced me to make the move to Toronto, as she had a job opportunity there. Suddenly, I was a country boy in an urban environment. It was a cultural shock, but I started to make the adjustment. In addition, I found a new job. We were building a new life, which included my wife furthering her education. Unfortunately, my wife decided she no longer wished to be married while completing her MBA. At the time, I was devastated, both emotionally and financially.

All of the investment properties and other assets of our marriage needed to be divided. I found myself in over $100,000 of debt by the time we completed the divorce. Thus 1997 was a year of great personal and financial change for me. I didn't give up my corporate job, but I did decide to take advantage of a monthly mentoring program with Raymond. The mentoring helped me to refocus on real estate and goal setting. Turning my mind to a more action-oriented focus meant that I started to feel less overwhelmed in the face of the huge upheavals that I had faced.

I borrowed money from my family. That loan helped me to make a down payment on my first new home after the divorce. I bought a cottage on Georgian Bay, near Parry Sound. At the same time, I continued to work and advance in the corporate world. The insurance of a steady paycheck allowed options. Over time, I started to purchase real estate again, growing my net worth. I was repairing my financial life, but also working on my emotional life as well.

I used the time immediately after my divorce to do my own personal soul searching. I spent time writing in my journal. I wrote almost daily about my feelings, my thoughts and my own mental state. I also took advantage of opportunities to travel. Keep in mind, I was a small town farm boy, who in the course of two years, had moved to the big city and began to travel around the world. I travelled across the USA, over to England, France, Germany, Italy, Switzerland, Africa – Malawi, the game park in Zambia and more. Before I was aware of the rest of the world, but it didn't impact me. Now I was learning that there is more out there that can have an impact on my life and where I was headed. But I needed to open myself up to the possibilities first.

It meant being willing to listen more and talk less. I had to experience life and allow myself to grow. This growth meant that I also experienced change in my personal life. I met Leanne in 1999 and we bought a house together. Over the next three years, I rebuilt my finances, getting out of debt and purchasing real estate investments, all while our relationship continued to grow. In 2002, we made it official and got married.

Investing in a Business

Real estate was my passive income, but I was still active in the corporate world. So when I was offered the opportunity to invest in an HVAC business, I took the chance to add this to my portfolio of passive income streams. I wanted to be sure that I wasn't dependent on just my paycheck, secure as it was.

Change was clearly marching through my life at this point. I had two children and while I was involved in their lives, it was evident that I was a working parent. Disconnecting from work was hard. So I needed to find a way to give back, primarily because I wanted to find a balance in my life. After all, I had come back from a traumatic emotional and financial experience to rebuild my net worth, but I felt that I may have neglected other aspects of my life. I first volunteered with the "big brother" organization. I found that time very rewarding.

Then I had an opportunity to start giving back in a profound way, starting with my national pastime – coaching hockey. At the same time, it also helped me to step outside of whatever might be going on in my own life to create a positive change in the lives of the young men that I have worked with throughout the years.

Coaching – Giving Back to Others Meant Helping Myself

As a Canadian, hockey was a part of my upbringing. I was always involved in playing it and while I wasn't going to the NHL, I definitely knew quite a bit about the game. Let's face it, hockey is the Canadian version of American football. Everyone has heard of it and a vast majority of kids have a working knowledge of the game, even if they aren't going to be star athletes.

Therefore, when the opportunity came, I decided to start coaching a team of 20 teen boys in the game of hockey. We made trips to the United States to play in tournaments, including Chicago. The tournaments meant I was chaperoning 20 teens with raging hormones. One of these tournaments was held in Chicago and on the same weekend as the Miss USA Teen pageant. Jason Spezza, who now plays hockey in Dallas, was along on that trip. Keeping those 20 young men focused on the game was hard to say the least.

Overall, more than 20 kids who I helped develop their hockey skills during their teen years have gone on to play in the NHL. Two were recent Toronto Maple Leafs, Daniel Winnick and Rich Clune. They evolved their skills during my coaching years with the Toronto Marlboros, building a foundation that helped them to grow into the players they are today.

This past year, I started coaching a very special player. My son joined my hockey team. For both of us, it was an adjustment. I was nervous the first time he skated onto the ice in front of the other kids on the team. I wondered if they were judging him and if they wondered about his skills and if he really belonged on the team. I was also afraid that I would set my expectations for him too high. He also wasn't sure at first how to take me as a coach. After all, at the rink, I yelled my instructions to be heard over the noise and throughout the large space. At home, as dad, I was fairly soft-spoken and quiet.

There was also the fact that we had to recognize that when the coach hat was on, the dad hat was off. Still, we found that it helped our relationship grow. Now we had opportunities to talk about various issues as we traveled back and forth to practices, games and tournaments. This one on one time helped our bond to deepen. I also noticed that our conversations naturally began to evolve to other topics beside hockey, including talking about business and life. Plus, seeing me in another role has given him more respect for me as a father. I have also begun to help him to understand how to adapt to change. Most change is really handled best through communication, which helps us to acclimate to new circumstances. At the same time, there have been plenty of times when I needed to reach out and seize the moment. This meant making a leap of faith, embracing the changes in my life. Action on my part meant that I felt empowered by change versus feeling helpless in the face of change.

As my children move into the teenage years, on a personal level, I find myself having to deal with changes again. Part of my new reality is that there are just a few years left before they are out of the house and moving on with their lives. But I am seizing the moments, making time for them and looking for ways to increase my family time. I seized the opportunity to become an author. Working with my personal mentor, Raymond Aaron, I have taken advantage of more opportunities, determined to make my life into what I want for myself and my family.

Change is a key to making your life amazing. Throughout this book, I will share with you lessons I have learned from the various major change points in my life, including those moments that felt like failures. As you read, I hope you take away how important it is to embrace change and use it to create momentum in your own life. So let's get started!

Chapter Two

Lessons Learned from My Three Major Failures

We all have moments in our lives when we just fail. It can be minor or it can be epic, but the point is that we have all done it. Failure doesn't have to be limited to just professional issues, but can happen in our personal lives as well. Family members or friends may part ways with us, and it can be devastating emotionally as we try to figure out what went wrong, but also if it is mendable or not. At the same time, these partings become changes in our lives that can propel us to go in a different direction than we ever expected. They can also lead us to meet individuals and encounter opportunities that we might not otherwise have experienced.

Still, no matter what type of failure we encounter, most of them carry with them some common areas where the relationship or business breaks down. These are five areas where I have consistently found my relationships or businesses fell apart. If you are committing these mistakes, then you will find that failure haunts your steps. So let's get started exploring these lessons I have learned from the three biggest failures in my life: my divorce, my partnership and my attempt at network marketing.

Lack of Communication

When it came to my first marriage, we sparked quickly, but on the communication level, we failed. What do I mean? We didn't really talk about our goals and dreams. We didn't talk with each other when times were tough. She didn't feel she could tell me about how she felt neglected and I couldn't make her see my sacrifice in terms of our move as a sign of my love and affection. The result is that over time, we became emotionally distant with each other. When she wanted to pursue her education and career opportunities, I went and packed up my life to move to the big city of Toronto. Yet our relationship did not improve, despite a change of scene. Our lack of a foundation and friendship meant that when she met someone whom she felt more compatible with in her MBA classes, she went after that relationship and left me behind.

There was nothing to repair, because we hadn't communicated and invested in each other. Here is the lesson for life and change: communicate. When you communicate with those you love, there is a foundation that is being built with them. Thus, big changes can have an impact, but they won't be able to rock the foundation. So many personal relationships fail when we stop talking to each other. Foundations of our relationships crack and fall apart, because the communication just stops. Do you have a relationship that you are neglecting in this respect?

The lack of communication is not limited to just personal relationships, such as those with family members or spouses. It can also bleed over into our relationships with those whom we work with. During my early years, I was always looking for ways to expand my family's net worth. After all, I didn't want to live on a paycheck to paycheck basis, but wanted to increase our income streams. My financial goals were focused on taking care of my family, but working smarter, not harder. It didn't always end up the way I planned.

I got into network marketing. Again, I ran into a lack of communication. In this case, I invested in a large amount of money into inventory, but hadn't done my homework. The business didn't come with a selling framework, but I was just encouraged to get more of my friends and family to buy the inventory. Eventually, I was left with a lot of inventory and a business failure, because no one wanted what I was selling. The company had received their share, however, so they weren't concerned about what I did with the goods now that I had them. Now I had to spend time and resources to get us out of the hole that was left from this business that never took off.

To say I was frustrated is an understatement. I wanted to create passive income for my family and build a real sense of positive change for us on a financial level. Instead, by not communicating my questions and striving to get answers, I had created a negative change in my life. But despite this rather harsh lesson in terms of business, I apparently still had not learned how important communication was. I was about to find out.

My business life presented an opportunity to be a silent partner in a business with a friend. The problem is that I didn't know how to communicate with my friend as a business partner, thus separating our business from our personal relationship. When I found out facts about the business that concerned me, I wasn't sure how to approach him and deal with the areas of the business that were struggling.

At the beginning, my trust in him as a friend also left me not asking critical questions about the business operations. Therefore, I didn't have the right information to make a truly informed decision about investing in this business. As the business relationship continued, our lack of meaningful communication continued to grow and had a profound impact. It also spilled over into our friendship, thus poisoning both wells at the same time.

In the end, the business relationship failed and we parted ways. Our friendship also suffered and we have not maintained our personal relationship at the same level. The lack of communication cost me in terms of relationships, as well as financially in terms of poor business decisions. While I might be able to recover the funds, the friendship and personal relationships were much harder changes and losses to swallow.

You can relate, I am sure, to one of the scenarios above. Although I am also sure that you could find many more examples throughout your personal and professional life. Think about those times where your communication suffered with a partner, friend or family member. Did it happen over time or was it due to a major life change? A lack of communication, regardless of when it happened, is often one of the key reasons for the failure within the relationship, or the souring of the business. How can you avoid the poison that comes from a lack of communication? We will discuss some ways to do so in the following chapters.

Lack of Research or Due Diligence

While this might seem to be a no brainer, there are many of us that make business or relationship decisions based just on our gut feelings, without taking the time to do our homework. In my business relationships, the failures were often because I didn't find myself in a position to ask those hard questions about how the business operated, what the numbers were and if the industry itself was thriving. I also avoided asking these hard questions, because I didn't want it to appear that I didn't trust the individuals that I would be investing with. I also didn't take the time to look at the sales framework and really understand how the money was earned in terms of generating leads and making sales.

Let's break that down first with my network marketing business. By not doing my due diligence on the business itself, I didn't understand at first that the business suffered from a lack of solid business planning. The whole point was to buy inventory and then convince more individuals to purchase inventory, become part of your network and thus allow you to earn commissions on your network. However, the business itself lacked a plan to get rid of the inventory. There was no training for individuals to sell or understand the products and in the end, there was little profit to be made. Instead, I was left with inventory that I couldn't sell and a network that wasn't making me any money.

Not to mention, there was the damage that was done to my reputation with the friends and family that had become part of my network, because they lost money as well. The impact of not doing my due diligence rippled beyond my own pocketbook.

Was it a financial failure? Absolutely! I had to learn that without the research, I was never going to have a successful business venture. Period! Money doesn't just come to us on trees in our backyard. It requires work and effort on our part to achieve success. Failing when it comes to business, often comes down to a lack of doing our own homework and truly understanding what we are getting into. Not everyone has the ability to really learn about how a business operates and what makes one successful or not, so they continue to fail time and time again. They don't improve their skill sets in terms of business investing and ownership, so they continue to crash and burn.

Then with each failure, they suffer a loss of some kind. It might just be financial, but it can also erode their confidence in business investing overtime. Enough losses and they stop trying to make the change in terms of their financial lives and attempting to meet their financial goals. Are you finding yourself in the position of wondering if you are just cursed in terms of finding that business where you can see a good return on your investment? Are your attempts at owning your own business not meeting any success?

If you are answering yes to any of these questions, then the next question is what kind of research did you do on the investment or business opportunity? If you are like me, you didn't do your homework at all or did a superficial investigation at best. You made a change to try to meet your financial goals, but it didn't work. Frustrating and time consuming as it may be, a lack of research and deep digging can make changes difficult and counterproductive. My partnership also crashed because I didn't get the information I needed at the beginning and we didn't support each other by keeping the information flowing between the two of us. Our personal relationship overshadowed the business relationship. I didn't feel comfortable asking for information about the business plan, sales goals, marketing and the financials, fearing that it would look as if I didn't trust my partner. In the end, my lack of willingness to ask for the financial and business data that I needed cost me the investment and my friendship.

As you can see, this lack of research doesn't stop at our business relationships. It can bleed into our personal relationships, both friendship and even our romantic ones. Take meeting someone new as an example. Romantic relationships often start with a spark, but with little thought about what our potential partner's real goals, dreams and desires are. We don't take the time to really make sure that our personalities are truly going to line up. The result is that we often reach a point where the spark is gone and there is nothing to back it up, because our communication didn't really focus on building a foundation that could support the relationship during times of stress or when facing challenges.

Over and over again, I was confronted with the reality of that lack of getting to know my ex-wife. She wanted different things than I did. If I had taken the time to learn more about her goals and dreams up front, we might not have gotten married, saving us both a lot of heartache. Does that mean that I didn't grow from these experiences? Absolutely not! The knowledge I gained from this relationship's ending impacted my future relationships, giving me more insight. If anything, the lessons reminded me that changes are all around us, and are happening on a constant basis. So it is important to look at how we are facing changes.

What is our mindset when confronted with a life partner or friend who asks more from us in terms of the relationship? Are we able to make the change needed to take the relationship to the next level? Or are our fears of change going to keep us from the potential joy and happiness that could result? Making our minds over in terms of how we view change can have a huge impact.

There are some individuals that fear change because of the unknown. Researching means that we are taking away the unknown by increasing our knowledge base. It is important to identify what scares you about change and work to mitigate it. Being proactive can make change feel less like a high speed train racing into your life. Instead, it can be prepared for and graciously invited into your life. The choice is really up to you.

Change is likely to be stressful and a negative experience if we don't take the time to communicate and learn about the person or the business. But there were more lessons for me to take away from these major life changes that I personally experienced. As I share the next few lessons, think about how you have made choices that are based on these lessons. Did you end up failing? Trust me, if you did, but if you internalize these lessons and built up your understanding and wisdom, then those failures can help you to make better choices down the road, turning change into a positive experience!

Didn't Make a Plan

For both my business and personal relationships, I often did not have a good plan to follow that would make the change a successful and positive one. While it might seem hard to think of romantic relationships in terms of a plan, it is important to have one. Working together, you and your partner need to come up with some goals for your relationship. Essentially, you need a plan.

If it's a romantic relationship, you need to ask those hard questions about what they see in their future. Do they want to raise a family or not? How would they want to raise children, if you had any? What are their financial goals? Are they saving and living within their means or do they struggle to keep with their budget? All of these questions are about building a plan for the future. Now let's be realistic. Life happens and it can mean that your plan has to be adjusted. But if you don't start out with one, then you have nothing to adjust, which can make it hard to maintain your relationship in the long run, as I found out.

But these types of questions may not work for a business relationship. So try different variations, which will help you to understand the business plan for the next few years. When will you be investing and for how long? What will be the rate of return? What are the potential risks and how are the business owners attempting to mitigate them? Does your investment translate into a percentage ownership? If so, how much of a voice do you have in the decision making process and if you do, what does that process look like?

It might seem that you are overthinking the investment or relationship, but the reality is without a plan and understanding of where the relationship or business is headed and the goals of the relationship or investment, then you will find that the change will have a negative taste In the long term. It is hard to stay motivated about a change and keep up your excitement when you aren't sure where you are headed or how you are going to get there.

I didn't have a plan for either one of my investments and so I wasn't able to focus my activity in a productive way. Spinning my wheels and not going anywhere. I am sure that you can imagine my frustration. But that level of frustration was topped by my anger and sadness at the end of my marriage. Six months of travel and meditation helped me to begin healing from that relationship ending. But again, I had no plan for how to make our relationship thrive. Thus, when it ended, we both dealt with accusations about what we could have done better, instead of feeling as if we had each given our all. Our relationship ending was a negative change and for me personally, it made it hard to start out in new relationships.

Not Taking Action

During my financial lifetime, I have attempted multiple businesses and not all of them ended in a successful sale and high return on my investment of capital, time and effort. In fact, sometimes a lack of action on my part was the reason that the change I tried to create had a negative result. One such business was my custom home building business.

When I first started this business, I was learning as I went. Originally, I just wanted to build my own custom home. So I started working away, designing my home and working with contractors to create my vision. Then my partner and I decided it was worth making into a business. Despite the fact that neither one of us had any experience in the home building business, because we had never run such an operation, we dove in.

Big surprise, we had a lot of major hiccups as we began the process. Our business was being run like two guys building a shed versus a business that managed inventory and the timeline for work to be completed, as well as a myriad of sub-contractors. This meant we were spending a lot of time and effort, but not really seeing any results for our work. Not only is a lack of action a big mistake, but action without a plan is also a wasted effort. When you act without a plan or don't act at all in the face of change, you can find your actions become wasted efforts that give change a bad taste in your mouth.

Your experiences shape your perspectives and beliefs. When you have a bad change experience, then that will impact how you view other changes, creating a snowball effect. The opposite is also true. When you have a positive change experience, it can make you more open to future change. Most of the lessons learned here are from actions I could have taken to make these positive changes in my life, but I didn't.

In my personal life, I noticed that things were not right between myself and my ex-wife. Yet, a part of me just figured that it would work itself out. Instead, the divide grew to the point that our marriage ended. Without defined actions in our personal relationships that are geared toward a purpose, then you will find that your relationships do not change in a positive way. Additionally, your relationship may struggle to adapt when life's circumstances have a greater impact, such as moving, building a home or the death of a loved one. Instead, they result in negative changes that can have a large emotional impact for years to come.

These impacts can make change a struggle and a frustrating experience for all those involved. Take a minute and think about how you personally have been impacted by a change. Did a lack of action on your part actually become the catalyst for the change occurring? When you can look at both major and minor changes with some distance and perspective, it can often be easy to pinpoint where our lack of action had a larger impact. But when we are in the midst of change, gaining that perspective can be very difficult to do. Hence, the reason we need outside perspectives from those that we know and trust. Mentors and life coaches can provide a great way to gain that perspective, especially when we are emotionally or financially invested in the change that is occurring, as I will discuss next.

Tony Debogorski

No Mentor Equals No Guide

No matter what choices and changes that we have dealt with in life, there are moments when we have reached out for guidance from a trusted professional or friend. Throughout these moments of failure in my life, it was clear that I was making choices without a mentor. I was relying heavily on my own wisdom and perspective, limited as it was. The reason that this can have a negative impact during a time of change is that we are emotionally invested in the current situation. So our perspective is dominated by how we are feeling, but not necessarily the knowledge, experience or skills we lack. It can be hard for us to look at the situation or change from another perspective. Thus, our decision making capability can be compromised.

Our personal relationships can also impact how we deal with and view change. For example, my friendship with my partner often clouded my ability to question him on business issues. Instead, I continued to just go along, without bringing more of a business perspective to the relationship. My inability to separate the two aspects of our relationship had a long term impact. Would it have been better if I had a mentor that could have pointed that out to me? The reality is that without those outside perspectives, we are all just making decisions based on our own judgement, experiences and emotions, but not necessarily all the information and understanding that we need.

Mentors don't just provide an outside perspective. They also provide a source of guidance that can help us to find our motivation to try a new path or make a major change. When I first answered Raymond's ad, I realized that he could be a source of guidance as I changed my financial life. However, his mentorship has impacted other areas of my life as well.

Do you have a mentor? Or do you find yourself being your own source of guidance? Are you frustrated with the results of the decisions you are making? If change is making you emotionally and physically drained, then you might find that you need to consider a mentor. Their skills and life experiences can give you a frame of reference to assist you in working through your own life experiences.

As humans, we crave some type of guidance. We look to our parents for guidance on how to live independently. Our friends also provide a touchstone in terms of whether or not we are progressing as individuals in society. Even when we look at our culture, there is built in rules that provide an area of guidance. Without some type of guidance or structure, we may learn how to function in society, but it can take longer and may often be harder as we must experience the lessons ourselves versus taking advantage of another individual's personal experiences and learning from them.

So it should be no surprise that guidance is what we look for during times of major change and upheaval. This is because we want to be reassured that we can survive this experience by looking to someone who already has. Does this mean that how we feel is going to match up exactly with those that we look to for guidance? No, but there is an opportunity for us to learn from them, both in how they reacted and the actions they took to move forward.

Look for mentors to follow and learn from. They can be in person or from afar, for a short time or a long time. I have followed many people from local to national to international. With the internet online blogs, radio talk shows and more, it is easier to follow the lead and expertise of more knowledgeable people than continue to try to forge a new path on your own.

As we talked about earlier, change is always happening, whether we like it or not. Therefore, we need to find ways to embrace change versus feeling attacked by it. As we will see in our next few chapters, the ability to make change a positive part of our lives is a key skill to living the life we want. Often, the lessons we learned from failures can be translated into a positive change going forward. So let's talk about the lessons I learned from some of the more successful changes in my life.

Chapter 3

Lessons Learned from my Three Major Successes

We have all experienced setbacks in our lives. These setbacks can often be the catalyst to embrace a major change or to kick off a major change in our lives. As you have seen, my life has been filled with some major life moments that were catalysts to major changes in my life. However, throughout these experiences, I have learned a lot about myself as a person. I have also come to realize that there is truly no way to anticipate change. The reality is that change is always occurring, in ways that are both large and small. To successfully deal with changes, there are 5 major lessons that I learned during some of the most successful changes in my life. No surprise, these lessons are based in growing my knowledge base, and always being open to learning from my mentors, friends and family. So let's dive into what I have learned during those times in my life where I successfully navigated change!

Don't Become Risk Adverse

Real estate is a constantly evolving industry, full of its own ups and downs. The last big recession, which started in 2008, was triggered by the housing industry's plunge downward. Clearly, it had a major economic impact and the ripples are still being felt in many areas of the world as economies work to recover and get back onto the growth track.

Tony Debogorski

My big real estate moment was actually triggered by my divorce. During this period of my life, all my real estate purchases were lost, as everything was sold to complete our divorce. I became a wanderer as I dealt with my emotions about the divorce and its emotional and financial impact. Yet I finally realized that I wanted to reinvest in real estate. I had seen my net worth grow before and I was determined that it would grow again.

It wasn't easy for me to make that leap. I was in a large amount of debt from the divorce, to the tune of over $100,000. Finding the money to invest in real estate was going to be a difficult task. So I turned to my family, who was willing to lend me the money for my down payment. This gave me the ability to purchase a cottage, which I used as my residence for a period of time. As I paid off debt, I was able to begin to purchase investment real estate again.

How many of you have had a major setback in your financial or emotional life? How did you deal with it? Did it hold you back from taking any risks in these areas? As humans, we all want to know what will happen next. Consistency is what we crave, even if we don't always want to admit it. Change can be hard especially when it comes with these types of impacts. When we deal with major emotional change, our response is to hold back to avoid feeling lost or abandoned again. The same could be said about our financial setbacks. We don't want to see our bank accounts take another hit, so we do our best to avoid risky investments, perhaps avoiding investing altogether. We are willing to do long term damage to our finances to avoid a possible loss, because we become risk adverse.

It might appear be easier to avoid potential financial risks, especially after we have suffered a major loss. This could be from a divorce, an investment that went wrong, or even a sudden influx of debt from a medical emergency or other unexpected disaster. Our initial response will most likely be that we do not want to take another risk like that. Yet if we are unwilling to learn from the financial mistake or setback and use that knowledge to move forward, then we are setting ourselves up to struggle in terms of growing ourselves and our net worth.

As we will discuss in Chapter 4, potential business opportunities to invest and grow our net worth are available through the internet, but only if we are willing to take a risk, instead of being risk adverse. But the only way to avoid becoming risk adverse is to see risk in a positive light. Changes have the best impact in our lives when we view them under a positive microscope. The reality is that our mindset has a large impact on how we view the changes that happen throughout our lives, both large and small.

Therefore, be willing to use setbacks in your finances or personal life to empower you to move forward. They should be times of self-assessment, but should not be a cause for us to shy away from what we perceive as risk. When we do so, we are putting ourselves in a position of missing out on greater opportunities that can help us to grow and create the lives that we want. Thus choosing to take risks can help us to make change work in our favor versus viewing change as a negative.

What are some ways to avoid become risk adverse? Here are just a few suggestions to help you break out of the risk adverse mentality and start embracing change.

1. **Try Something New** – The reality is that those who are risk adverse stop looking for new opportunities and ways to grow their personal experiences and knowledge base. When we stop being willing to try new things, but instead prefer to stay in our comfort zone, we put ourselves into a position where change becomes very scary thing. Be willing to bust out of that routine by exploring new experiences. It will keep you from becoming so risk adverse that change becomes something to fear versus something to embrace.

2. **Decide Your Outlook** – Instead of looking for the negative in each new experience, look for the positive. When you make a change in your outlook, you may find it easier to embrace other changes, even those that on the surface might bring negatives into your life. It has often been said that a majority of what happens to us depends less on the circumstances and more on our outlook regarding the circumstances. Changing our outlook can often have a positive impact on how we view change.

3. **Make a Goal and then Follow Through** – Goals have always been a great way to fight your fear of change and risk. The reason is that you have a plan to move forward, which can make it easier to embrace a change. Setting goals and creating a plan also helps you to build up your knowledge base. Remember our fear of change can come from a fear of the unknown. By increasing our knowledge of a subject, we decrease the unknown, which can reduce our fear or sense of risk aversion.

4. **Appreciation of the Little Things** – We have all heard the various sayings that are geared toward helping us to appreciate various aspects of our lives. When we become risk adverse, our world shrinks and it can become hard to really appreciate those blessings in our lives. Therefore, it is important to take the time to appreciate what we have around us, including family, friends and even nature. Doing so can help to remind us of the wider world, because those small things can remind us of the bigger picture.

As you can see, the most important thing to remember is that risk aversion is a state of mind. We have the ability to change our state of mind, but if we aren't willing to make the effort, then we are not going to see the results that we expect. Next, we are going to look at some of the other lessons I have learned from some of the positive major changes in my life. You can take these lessons and apply them to your life to help you grow in your ability to create positive change and embrace change overall.

Communication is Key!

When we talked about the lessons that I learned from my greatest failures, those lessons left me empowered to move forward. Communication was one of those lessons. While I was in a place where I wasn't communicating with my partners and my ex-wife, changes in my life resulted in major setbacks. I couldn't help but wonder why this was happening to me, when in fact, I should have been asking why it hadn't happened sooner.

Communication is that critical. Without it, major misunderstandings can occur in our lives to the point that we are creating our own setbacks. The financial impact can be major, as was the case with my business partnership. However, a lack of communication can have a greater impact on our personal relationships, especially those that are closest to us.

When those hard times come, our ability to communicate with those who are closest to us can have a profound impact on how we weather those changes and difficult circumstances. Have you ever dealt with a difficult circumstance and felt isolated from those around you? Have you felt as if you have a lack of support as a result? In part, that isolated feeling is due to the inability to communicate your feelings and how the circumstances are affecting you with those family and friends. You also aren't open to the support that they may be able to offer you, because you have closed yourself off.

Since communication is so critical to our lives, the question becomes how can we improve communication in key areas of our lives. Let's start with the non-verbal communication. Whether you realize it or not, your body is constantly giving off communication cues to those around you. Crossing your arms during a discussion? You could be coming across as unwilling to really listen to your companion's point of view. Telling someone you are listening, but not really engaging them by looking at them in the face and focusing on them? This could be sending off a signal that you do not think what they have to say is important.

When you are dealing with others, it is important to make sure that your non-verbal cues match what you are saying to the important people in your life. Even if you are just having a conversation with the grocer or service personnel, taking the time to focus directly on them can help you engage and at the same time, show appreciation for their hard work in your behalf. When we have a major change in our lives, our non-verbal cues can also tell those around us how the change is affecting us. If we tend to use non-verbal cues that appear to close us off from others, it could be a sign that we are letting the change negatively impact us.

Communication at work and home are two of the most critical areas in our lives. Misunderstanding due to poor communication cues with your workmates can create a tense situation that can limit productivity. At the same time, our personal relationships can suffer as we find ourselves frustrated because our life partners and family members don't understand us.

Therefore, take the time to give yourself a critical communication test. Ask yourself what types of signals that you are giving off during your conversations with others. If you find that your cues are giving off a closed appearance to others, work on relaxing before a discussion. This could mean taking a deep breath, taking your hands out of your pockets and putting a smile on your face. Do things that allow you to internally relax and then your non-verbal cues will begin to reflect that relaxed state.

Taking a moment to relax can also assist you in communicating when the topic is a difficult or sensitive one. By getting our mind into a more relaxed state, we can find it easier to listen as well as to be heard. What might have been a difficult discussion may go much easier than we expect. But even if it doesn't, we will be able to take the results of the discussion better if we take the time to relax ourselves.

During a discussion, don't be afraid to ask questions. Also, take the time to repeat back the answers in your own words. Doing so will let the individual you are talking with know that you are paying attention and that you understand what they just said. It also demonstrates that you are interested in what they are saying. Questions can also be a great way to draw someone into a conversation, allowing you to learn more about them. If you are discussing a new investment, questions can help you learn about the investment and the business plan. This is something I didn't do with my initial partnership and I suffered the financial consequences of that choice.

When it comes to our personal relationships, however, communication takes on a whole new level. Questions help you to understand the point of view of the other person, really getting to the heart of what could be creating a divide. These questions can also help you to build a foundation of knowledge about the other person. At the same time, good communication allows you to emotionally support each other through the variety of life's experiences. Your approach during these moments can make your partner feel attacked and defensive. On the other hand, communication, which is focused on creating a positive change and finding solutions versus accusing the other person and listing what they did wrong, will always have a more positive outcome in the long run. Additionally, the other person will feel your support, instead of a feeling of judgment.

Communication gives you the ability to invest in the people in your life, drawing closer to them over shared experiences or just sharing the various aspects of your lives with each other. Change comes to everyone, but the question is will you have to deal with change feeling alone? Or can you make the changes to how you communicate so that you can see your friends and family rally to support you? Building our relationships mean dwelling on our foundations with others and shoring them up with good communication.

Finally, it is important to make sure that we are practicing good listening skills. Communication is more about how well we listen to what others are saying to us than it is about what we say. So take the time to really listen, not just preparing your next point as the other person talks. Take the time to process what they are saying to you, even repeating it back before you respond. There is an old saying that we were given two ears but only one mouth, meaning that we are meant to listen more than we speak.

Look at your most successful relationships. If you analyze them, you will find that those relationships are benefiting from your best listening skills. For those relationships that don't seem to be doing as well, it might be worth asking yourself how much you are listening and how well you are listening. A change in how you listen might have a larger impact than you might realize.

I made the effort to be a better communicator and one the blessings for that change was that I met my current wife. Our foundation is stronger because I realized that I really had to talk to her about my goals and dreams, making sure that they were compatible with hers. As I got to know her on a deeper level, I was building a foundation of honest communication that led to our relationship getting stronger and my feelings for her becoming stronger as a result. Once we made it official, that deep level of communication only continued to make our relationship stronger. Years later, we can still talk honestly with each other about our family, our goals and how changes are impacting our relationship.

When you are choosing a significant other, it is easy for us to let our hearts take over, pushing honest communication about potential red flags in the relationship on the back burner. But in the long run, that can be a choice with larger emotional consequences. Change comes to us all, but how we communicate can have a large impact on how that change can be viewed, either positively or negatively. But communication goes hand and hand with our willingness to do our due diligence or research, which we will discuss next.

Do Your Homework!

No matter if it is a new personal relationship or a new investment, it is critical that we make an informed decision. The only way to do that is to take the time to do our homework. When it comes to business investments, this means taking the time to do the research on the business, its industry and ask questions about the numbers. If the industry numbers indicate a certain profit level, but the business you are considering has a number far outside of the range, you may need to reconsider investing in the business.

Also, it is important to read through the contract. Look for clauses about how much decision making ability you will have in trade for your investment. The fine print can often bring the biggest surprises. If you are considering making a major change in your life using an investment, then you need to really consider all the angles. As I found out, it is important to know more about the business itself than to just to make a decision based on faith or a friendship. Business relationships can have an impact on the personal relationships, especially if individual roles within the business or investment are not clearly defined at the start.

Mentors can also play a role here, because they can help you to ask the questions that you might not have considered. But do not think that mentors are limited strictly to your career and business relationships. In fact, a mentor can assist you in asking the right questions of a potential life partner. When we discussed the importance of communication, I pointed out how we got to know each other over time. In many ways, we were both doing our homework, researching each other's personality traits, goals and life experiences. Our relationship is much closer as a result.

The types of mentors available for your personal life can be ministers, pastors, counselors or life coaches. The point is that with every shift we make in our lives, there are those who have gone before us and can provide guidance, perspective and suggestions to make the path we are walking easier.

When you encounter dramatic changes in your life, the ability to do research can help you to cope with the change itself. This can include medical news, economic news or even technological changes. Empowering yourself often begins by gaining more knowledge. That leads me to the next lesson, continuing your education.

Constantly Learning

The reality for most of us is that change is scary, because it is the unknown. As humans, we like to know what is going to happen next. The unexpected can be scary and frightening, as it can seem to bring negative consequences into our lives. A medical diagnosis is often not greeted with joy, but is often found to bring a negative impact on our family, work and personal lives. So the question is how can we combat the fear of unknown? Simply put, we need to work hard at growing our own personal knowledge base. This means that when a change occurs in our lives, we want to take the time to learn more about the impactful circumstances. In the case of a medical diagnosis, learning more about the disease and its impact can help us to deal with the challenges of the diagnosis.

Throughout the many challenges of my life, from a business investment that failed to work out or my personal struggles, I have always found that continuing to grow my education has helped me to cope with the challenges and obstacles that I am confronted with on a daily basis. The act of learning about something takes away the mystery of the situation and can actually help me to relax as I face the challenge or problem. So how do you view education? Do you see it as a means to complete high school or college and then you are done? Or do you see education as a life-long pursuit that can help you to grow as an individual and at the same time, help you to deal effectively with change?

Throughout the years, I have seen a great deal of change in terms of technology. The Internet was in its infancy less than 20 years ago. Today, we rely on it for virtually everything, from ordering basic supplies to speaking with family around the world. The impact on business in terms of reviews cannot be underrated as well. There are so many ways that the Internet has become a part of our everyday lives. Yet, there are some who find the Internet intimidating and would rather continue to do things "just as we always have." Not only does this demonstrate an unwillingness to change, it also shows how our willingness to learn a new skill or topic can impact how well we embrace change. Educating yourself can mean finding mentors, taking classes or even just going to your local library and exploring the variety of books on multiple topics that are available there. Being open to new ideas and ways of completing tasks can also help you to grow your knowledge base. Overtime, you might be surprised at how your viewpoint on change has been altered, just by increasing your knowledge base.

Additionally, when we build a larger knowledge base, we may find new hobbies or activities that we enjoy, which we might otherwise have missed out on. Do you have a favorite hobby that you enjoy, such as fishing? Perhaps when you first started out, you didn't catch a fish right away. Or you might have struggled to clean your fish properly. But as your knowledge grew, so did your ability. Overtime, you found yourself able to do these things and so much more. Thus, your enjoyment of fishing only grew.

The Internet has provided us the same ability. Family, for example, can be separated by distance, but using online calling, you can quickly see and hear them. Activities no longer have to be limited just because someone lives far away. But if we are not willing to take the time to learn how to use these technological offerings, then we can miss out on the benefits that they offer us to keep in contact with our families and friends.

As you can see, technological changes can also mean that we have opportunities to increase our income stream. Before the Internet took off, we were limited in how we could build an income stream, either passive or active. For those who were willing to invest the time and money, a brick and mortar business was the only option to really grow your income because you were now your own boss. You could also choose to invest, but investments were often risky and losses could be major setbacks financially.

Plus, there are all the inherent challenges in opening your own business, in terms of being able to reach your target audience in your geographical area and at the same time, managing large amounts of overhead and startup costs. Thus, many individuals found themselves limited to working as the employee versus the employer, because starting their own business was too cost prohibitive.

The Internet has changed that in a big way. All of a sudden, the little guy with a smaller amount of capital can start their own business. These businesses aren't limited to a geographical area or a small target audience. Instead, you have access to a global audience, but often do not have to spend a large amount to hire employees, stock inventory or maintain a brick and mortar store.

Great, you might be saying, I want to tap into that. But it requires that you need to spend time building your knowledge of how the Internet works and doing your homework before investing in a business. After all, not all Internet business opportunities are created equal. Some might be nothing more than a clever scheme to part you from your money. However, you have to take an opportunity to educate yourself and avoid falling victim to a scam. Continuing education is key to creating and navigating change in your life, both professionally and personally.

Change comes in the form of decisions that we have to make, understanding that it is impossible to take two paths at the same time. Therefore, by our willingness to never stop learning and growing, we can build a life that is full of change that we can view as enriching and that we are willing to embrace as it comes. Now that we are taking steps to make change that occurs in our lives a more positive experience, let's look at how we can take steps to create change in our own lives, changes that will impact us in ways that we anticipate and some that we never expect.

Make a Plan and Take Action

Throughout my life, I have had opportunities to look at my life and decide I didn't like the direction that it was heading. When my divorce occurred, I didn't like how I felt and I needed a change. So I took the opportunity to travel for six months. Yes, I was dealing with a mountain load of debt and other issues, but my mental health was even more important. I didn't really have a plan, but it gave me a chance to reflect on my life and what I wanted to do next.

The point is that I took action. I was willing to do something to change the status quo of my life after such an emotional and personal adjustment. Did that mean that I was perfectly ready to jump into another relationship after I got back from my travels? No, it wasn't really that simple, but I found that after I was done, I had made some great strides emotionally. I felt ready to start tackling the issues that I had left behind, including that mountain of debt.

When it comes to dealing with change, often the worst thing you can do is nothing at all. Action breeds forward motion, which is key to making change work in your favor. No matter what is happening in your life, it is important to make sure that you are moving yourself forward. So what does a forward direction look like? It can mean moving toward your goals, learning from a failure or even continuing your education through new experiences. Instead of being the naysayer, it is key to keep asking yourself what you can do to make this a better experience or help you to learn from it to grow personally, professionally or spiritually.

We all have moments when we find ourselves asking why such a circumstance occurred to us and our loved ones. Yet in the midst of a circumstance that is a large and traumatic change, we can still take action and make a plan. At these moments, we can't control the circumstances, but we can control how we react to them. So what type of plan can we implement with change? Depending on the change, the plan might be a list of to-do items, altering our routine or even how we interact with ourselves and others. In other cases, it may mean setting up a budget and a list of goals to reduce or eliminate debt. Other goals can require different plans, but our willingness to go forward with our continuing education can help us to create an action plan that will match our goals, no matter what circumstances they may be in response to.

When I was faced with a large sum of debt from my divorce, dealing with it meant working and paying it off. I created a plan of payments and goals that allowed me to see forward progress, while at the same time keeping me motivated as I worked to pay off everything. The days were not always easy, but the change in my circumstances was easier to take because I was taking action and I had a plan to move forward. I didn't feel like a victim of my circumstances, but as an active participant in them.

For many of us, change can mean feeling out of control in our own lives, which can trigger our fear and risk aversion responses. By creating an action plan, we can feel more in control, despite the changes that we might be going through and the challenges that we may be facing.

Still, I didn't have all the answers to everything that I was dealing with. While I did take the time to study and learn, it was also key to find a coach or mentor to assist me in moving forward.

Find a Mentor for Guidance

Let's go back to the sport analogy for a moment. When we first start learning a sport, no matter what it is, we do not know everything. Most of the time, we don't know the rules of the game, the appropriate moves, and even what would be considered a foul or not appropriate plays within the game. I have coached hockey for years and during that time, I have worked with kids who have a various degrees of experience when it comes to hockey. Yet all of them could improve their skill level through listening to my coaching and putting my experience and knowledge to use.

What is a mentor? Let's stop for a moment and define what that really means by looking at a few of the differences between a mentor and a coach.

When it comes to coaching, there is typically a specific task involved. The focus tends to be on concrete issues or challenges, so the focus of the coach is teaching the skills to meet the needs created by those issues or challenges. On the other hand, mentoring is more relationship based. Therefore, an individual seeking a mentor is looking for more than just a new skill set, but a relationship that can address a variety of areas within one's life.

Coaching is also usually short term, as the coach imparts the necessary information and then moves on. A mentor, however, may be in their mentoree's life for years at a time. This is because they are building a relationship on trust and that takes time. I have had a long relationship with Raymond and he continues to serve as a mentor to me.

Tony Debogorski

As someone who has served as a coach for many years, I know that coaching itself doesn't require much in the way of a design or plan. After all, if you know about a topic, you can easily pass your knowledge along in a relatively short period of time. On the other hand, mentoring is a relationship that is designed to determine the strategic purpose for mentoring, what will be the focus areas, the specific mentoring models and the components that will guide the relationship. This can often be true when finding a mentor to match with a mentoree.

One of the key parts of coaching is that it is typically performance driven. After all, once a coach has imparted the necessary skills or knowledge, then the coaching relationship typically ends. In hockey, it is usually year to year, then the next group comes along. Mentoring, on the other hand, is more development driven. The purpose is to help an individual develop not only for the current goals, but to meet future ones as well.

As you can see, mentoring focuses more on the development of an individual as a whole. Coaching, on the other hand, is more results driven and skills-oriented. Therefore, while a coach might see more instant results, a mentor will have a longer term impact on an individual because of the relationship that they will have built with each other. You could meet someone who could be both a coach and a mentor as well.

In our own lives, the reality is that we don't know everything. Finding coaches and mentors can help us to grow in terms of our professional and personal lives. The reason is that we are able to take advantage of their experiences and knowledge to provide guidance and perspective as we navigate change. They can also help us to implement change in our own lives by encouraging action and helping us to create a plan, then holding us accountable for following through on the milestones and goals that make up the plan.

However, I want to note here that not every mentor will stick with you throughout your life. In fact, you may find that you have several mentors at the same time. Each of them will provide an experience or point of view that you can draw on. Years ago, I answered that ad for Raymond Aaron and went to a seminar where he was the featured speaker. It turned out to be the first of many. Over the years, his straight talking advice and point of view has given me the ability to make changes in my life, because he cuts through the excuses that I can come up with.

Let's be realistic. We all can create excuses of why we aren't moving forward on a path or why it is too hard to deal with a specific change in our lives. Those excuses give us the ability to focus on what is wrong with the change and why we can't move forward. This means we can use the victim mentality to keep ourselves stagnant. We use excuses to allow us to avoid taking action regarding the change and its impact on our lives. Excuses allow us to procrastinate, which ultimately leads nowhere.

Mentors and coaches can call us out when we are making excuses that are stopping our forward progress. They make us take those hard looks at ourselves and our internal dialogue. As a result, they make us want to try to move forward, while motivating us to take action that we might not have been willing to take without the benefit of our mentors.

How many of us have heard about large companies that create a mentoring program? The point of these programs is to assist their most promising employees to grow their professional skills and experience. With this growth, it is hoped that opportunities will come for them to advance within their careers, while staying with the company. The leadership hope that the company will be stronger as a result, because they will have developed their employees as people, instead of just giving them a few new skills before forcing them to move on.

In many ways, we can create our own mentoring program. Learn what you can from each mentor as you encounter them. Then be willing to search for additional mentors as you grow in your skills and experiences. The point of mentors is that they can assist you to grow and change. Once you have grown and learned from someone, it now puts you in the position of being able to mentor someone else. At the same time, you are coming into a position of being more whole as an individual, because you are continuing your education throughout the course of your life.

However, it is important to never stop looking for mentors and coaches, assuming that we no longer need them. After all, the point of life is to keep growing. Change actually helps us to achieve that growth by forcing us out of our comfort zones. Mentors can also help us to reach outside of our normal to see different possibilities outside of our current level of experience.

Take that to your financial life. Mentors can often help you to learn and explore income options outside of your own personal experience. This includes how to understand how different types of businesses will match your strengths and areas where you need to learn or expand your skills in order to be successful. No one starts a business knowing everything to make it a success. Often, we just jump in with a business plan and learn as we go. Exploring different business opportunities can help us to make a more informed leap, so to speak. One area that I have begun to explore is building a business online. After all, like so many of you, I want to be able to live a life that isn't tied to a traditional job with a defined schedule. I want to be available for my children and my family. Life is about experiences and I want to be able to have as many of them as possible with those who are closest to me.

As I have looked for opportunities that provide the financial income needed to give me that freedom, I have worked with my mentors to identify opportunities. One of these was real estate investments, but online businesses bring a whole new level to my financial world. After all, this is an opportunity to make money through a global audience that is online 24 hours a day. I could be making money even when I am sleeping, which is an attractive income stream indeed.

One of my mentors is a man named Matt. He started a business that capitalized on the global audience available through the internet. In the next chapter, I will explore the benefits of his business model and what it entails. This particular change in my life has me excited and I hope it empowers you to consider a financial change of your own!

Chapter 4

My Newest Success

When it comes to our financial success, there is often an idea of where we want to be, but not necessarily a true path to get there. So the question is how to create a new source of income that can support the life we want to lead versus the life we are living now. At the same time, it needs to support our lifestyle, not become our lifestyle.

With a quality mentor, you can avail yourself of a different point of view, which gives you the ability to gather the information you need to make a critical decision about the type of business that will work for you. For me, Matt provides a mentoring aspect that helped me to work my way through the various aspects of an Internet business, particularly one that is a franchise or affiliate opportunity. Before I share with you how this business works, let's explore how a brick and mortar business works and the benefits of a franchise business.

Brick and Mortar: Tied Down Lifestyle

When you first open a new business, there are a variety of things to keep in mind. You have to develop a product or service that can then be reproduced and sold to a target audience. Based on the geographical area, your location may or may not be able to capture the right target audience for your product or service. Then you will need to build a brand, find a location, hire employees, train them, set up your bookkeeping, track startup costs and a myriad of other tasks that define starting a business.

Creating a product or service involves a lot of research, trial and error, as well as defining who your target audience is for your product or service. Then there is the effort that is involved to find a manufacturer that produces the product at your quality level. If you are providing a service, then you need to create a training manual and a system that can train your employees to deliver the service to your expected quality level. After all, high quality product and services can demand top dollar pricing for your business.

Yet the work of a brick and mortar business does not stop when open the doors for the first time. There is the ongoing marketing, as well as the hours that must be put in keeping the doors open and managing the inventory involved. As you can see, the amount of effort that need to be put into a brick and mortar business is extensive. Even after all that work, it is still possible that the whole business could end up closing and be deemed a failure because your target audience was not based in your geographical area.

There is clearly a lot that goes into a brick and mortar business. The lifestyle is one that you need to keep working constantly and the brick and mortar location ties you down as a result. Hours must be kept to and you are limited in terms of your ability to make money from the business based on those hours and the flow of potential customers. Overhead is also consistent, even if the income is not.

Internet businesses, on the other hand, are not limited in this regard. Your business can be earning money constantly, because a website never has to close. Plus, your target audience does not need to dwell in your geographical area. You suddenly have a global audience, which can help you to increase your sales and the reach of your brand. Additionally, the overhead costs are significantly less than a brick and mortar enterprise. Thus, your profit can be significantly higher, even if you don't make as many sales.

As you can see, a brick and mortar business can be a complicated and time consuming process. If your life goal is to have more time for your family, this route may end up taking you further away from your goal. Often, the people you want to see and spend time with are the ones that you spend the least amount of time with because you are focused on being physically present at the store.

If you are choosing to franchise, then you might be taking more of a calculated risk. After all, most franchise opportunities mean that the company has done the work for you. They have developed the product or service. The company will also have created a training manual and marketing plan. If you follow what they have laid out, then you can be successful. Still, you are limited to the hours that you can be open at your brick and mortar store. In addition, you have to follow the franchise model, even if you see another opportunity that could enrich your store or potentially expand your marketing reach.

Therefore, we can definitely say that the brick and mortar business plan has some benefits, but it also has some definite limitations in terms of the money that can be made and the work that is involved. But at the same time, the internet provides the ability to take the benefits of a brick and mortar, but expand them beyond one geographical location. Your franchised products are available constantly to your target market. The ability to reach out and tailor your marketing in terms of pay-per-click advertising and other options can also help you to grow in terms of what your business can be. So let's explore the type of business that I encountered when I first met Matt.

What Makes Internet Marketing a Perfect Business Model?

Matt's online business that allows individuals to franchise a business with high quality products that provide a significant value to your customers. But what makes this business different from the variety of business options that are available on the internet? When it comes to choosing an online franchise business model, you should be looking for a model that provides a comprehensive training program with proven products that work for your customers and keep them coming back again and again. For a brick and mortar franchise, you are looking for a business that provides a quality product that will appeal to your customers. After all, the lifeline of almost any business is a repeat customer. Typically, it is cheaper to reinvest in a previous customer than to spend money trying to bring in new customers.

This is where Matt really stands out. His online business model produces high quality products that are beneficial to their customers. But they are also able to sell those products to your customers over and over again, thus allowing your online franchise business to grow and grow. Depending on the specifics of your particular online business, you may be paid a commission for leads you provide or a commission based on the sales that you make yourself. But either way, the best business model is one that provides you a way to plug into their success, thus making an investment for the long term with plenty of benefits because you can avoid the mistakes that you might make when starting a business from scratch.

Matt provides a "Done For You" business model as we have discussed throughout this book. This means that they have already created the products, the training, the marketing platform and other necessary parts of the business. As a franchise license holder, you get to benefit from having this program completely ready for you. All you have to do is plug in and follow the training to bring in your leads. As you bring in those leads, you can then begin to make commissions off those sales.

Overtime, your leads become repeat customers that make more purchases of these high quality products. As a result, the profits and commissions from one sale are significantly higher than those that are made from multiple sales. Plus, you aren't the one who actually has to make the sales or stock inventory to tracked, shipped and guaranteed. Instead, you are just providing leads to quality sales people who take over from there.

Does that mean you will be making sales every day? It depends on the quality of your leads. But the point that you need to keep in mind is that you will be making a significantly higher profit on the sales that are made to your leads. Your return on investment is significantly higher as a result.

In the world of marketing, leverage is often defined as the use of a small initial investment to reap a relatively high return. While you might have a great product or service, that is no longer enough to win over your potential buyers and turn them into customers. After all, most individuals are literally bombarded on a daily basis with marketing materials, from all types of media.

Therefore, you need to use your resources in such a way that you cut through the clutter that your potential buyer is dealing with, making your product or service stand out from the crowd. Plus, you have to do this with a relatively small budget and perhaps limited resources. So how can you reach your target audience effectively? With a franchise business, they should provide a sales funnel as part of your system to assist you in your marketing efforts. If they do, you will notice a message that is clear and positions your business.

When you are creating your messaging, it is important to remember that you want to get to the point. Your audience will quickly lose interest if they can't see in a few seconds why this email is important to them. Your sales tools must also show the customer why the products you are offering are worth the cost and how they would be valuable to them. If the message wanders off point, then it is hard for you to grab the buying audience that you are looking to attract.

When most individuals think of leverage, they are trying to find a means to market their product to their target audience but on a minimal budget. Essentially, they are looking for a large marketing return for a minimal investment. While this type of "free" leverage might bring some sales, it cannot be considered a permanent or effective strategy to build sales for the long term.

Additionally, you want to make sure that any leverage you choose for your marketing message does not lower the value of the products and services that you offer. For example, if you are setting up sales frequently as part of your leverage marketing, you may find that your target audience ends up missing the value of your products. Offers should enhance the value of your products versus diminishing them.

Ultimately, it is important to find a way to build your leverage so that you connect with the right people at the right time to get the best results possible. So let's discuss one method of getting the right people on your site at the right time, through the purchasing of web traffic.

When it comes to starting a new business, there is the assumption that free is the best route, because it reduces the overall startup costs that a new business incurs. You could feel much the same way in regards to your new business. Your train of thought could go something like this:

"I have a Facebook (or Twitter) account. I post about my own life; I should be able to create quality posts for my business. Then I get my friends to share them and I can drive traffic to my website and my business will grow."

Now while that sounds great in theory, the reality is that marketers are good at their job for a reason. They know how to get posts out to the right audiences and to grow your potential customer base. When you depend on organic growth, it can be a struggle to move your business to the next level. It may take twice as long to build your audience. Another point to keep in mind is that organic free growth is not targeted or leveraged growth. It is just organic traffic, which means that it has swept up a lot of individuals who are not going to purchase your products, but are essentially taking up time and effort on your part or bandwidth on your website.

While your website can handle a large number of views, the important views are the ones that actually end up making a purchase. The question is, did your free and organic growth really reach buyers or just give your website a bunch of views?

Paid traffic, on the other hand, is targeted traffic. These individuals can come to your website through well placed ads or pay per click advertisements. The ad platform matches your ad to the right audience and puts it onto the websites that audience visits regularly.

Does this mean that you should not take advantage of free traffic? While we don't encourage anyone to turn away this free and organic traffic, the reality is that it may not contribute much to your bottom line. You essentially get what you pay for. If you aren't paying to target your buyers and get them to your site, you may not turn the profits you expect and make it harder to cover your costs in the long run.

So how can you buy traffic or drive your targeted audience to your site? The reality is that there is no easy way to arrange for people to come to your website and make a purchase. One of the most successful ways to reach your target audience is through pay per click ad campaigns. The benefits of these types of ad campaigns is that they do not cost you anything unless an individual clicks through to your website.

Therefore, you can build your own campaign, target your visitors based on specific keywords and then implement your budget by bidding on those keywords. Many of the sites that allow you to make this type of targeted purchase will allow you to manage your campaign, dropping keywords that are less effective and truly customize your ads. You can even see the type of consumer that is coming to your side based on specific ads.

Your products can then begin to speak for themselves. However, since this is money that you are spending to drive traffic, it is important to make sure that you are continually updating the campaigns to get the most benefit from them over time. Use the PPC campaign to get the traffic and then use the statistics to see what the traffic does and if they turn into buyers or not.

As you can see, online marketing is a continual strategic effort that requires refining throughout your ad campaign. If your online business is not seeing the growth that you expect, it might be time to revisit your strategy. However, you should note that online business advertising is going to cost the same regardless of whether you have low cost products or high cost products. In the end, the same amount of advertising effort can go into both types of products, but only one will bring greater overall profit in the long run with less conversions of buyers. That is working with high quality and high value products that can make you more profit with just a few sales. Work smarter, not harder. The result can be a positive financial change.

Remember when we discussed leverage and all that it entailed? We repeatedly pointed out that it is worth spending the funding to drive targeted leads to your website, especially if those leads are being sold higher quality products with a higher profit margin. Matt does that same type of leverage, teaching you how to bring in those targeted leads that are more likely to turn into long term customers, ones that will make you money again and again.

It is important to note here that some online business will pay commissions on the initial sale, but any sales after that are not credited to you as a franchise or affiliate. This means that you need to continue producing leads over and over again. Remember how I talked about the cost of a new customer versus a repeat customer? As you continue to build your network of leads, you want to be sure that you are not continuing to spend the money to find the new leads, with no profits from the repeat customers that were once your leads.

Matt's business allows you a commission off of sales that are made to the leads you bring in, every time a sale is made to them. That's right, even the repeat sales. Which means when you have an initial investment to find that lead, you are going to see that lead continue to be profitable long after you have spent that initial investment. I love the idea of a lead working for my business long after I have recouped my initial investment to locate them and build them into my network.

Does that mean that any business with a similar platform to Matt's will be successful? It depends on their platform and who they have involved in their business. If you know who you are dealing with, it can make you either more confident in their business model or it can make you warier. Therefore, it is important to get to know the company and the people that run it before you make your initial investment.

So who are the people behind this business and how can that help you to build confidence in the brand itself?

thebookofchangenow.com

Making a Change by Knowing the Brand

Matt began his business with the idea that being wealthy is a change in mindset. When you examine who controls the wealth in this world, a vast majority of them own a business or multiple businesses. This means that if you want to truly build your net worth and grow a source of income over time, then you need to become a business owner as well. Does this mean that you will always have success? Not necessarily, but that is the reality of business. Yet if you choose to take on a franchise business and follow their model and training, you greatly increase the likelihood of your business being successful over the long term, both in profitability and longevity.

Matt took this idea of business ownership and started to build an array of high quality products, a marketing strategy, a quality sales force and a consistent delivery system. Then he began to reach out to others, offering a partnership or franchise opportunity that would bring in more leads to match customers with his products.

As a result, Matt's business has continued to grow and find success. Commissions have been paid out consistently as the company continues to expand. The products offered vary widely, but the main message is that they are meant to improve the lives of the customers who purchase them, providing value with every high quality product.

But Matt also saw an opportunity to provide mentors and coaching to those who wanted to make a change for the better in terms of their financial well-being and life goals, but who didn't know how they were going to get there. Thus, Matt provides a coach to their franchise partners, allowing them to benefit from the coach's knowledge to answer questions and give them guidance as they start their online business. Thus, the business is built to be an opportunity for those who are just starting out, but also a support system for those who have continued to work their businesses and are looking to grow beyond their current income level.

Matt's online business provides opportunities to grow your income, but also to make changes in your own life to live the way that you want to. At the same time, you aren't tied to the brick and mortar franchise that puts you in the position of hiring staff and keeping to specific hours. In fact, you don't even have to manage inventory. The benefits of these products is tied to the fact that the products are high value and high quality, so they speak to your potential customers' needs.

Here is a quick business lesson. If you want to make $100 from selling your products, then you are going to have to a set number of products to sell based on your product type. Low priced products are going to sell quickly, but the profit margin on them is lower as a result. If you sell a product for a $1, and you receive $.10 cents in profit, then you will need to sell 1,000 of your product to reach $100. On the other hand, if you sell a product that is worth $10, with a profit margin of a $1, then you can reach that number with only 100 sales. Big difference in the amount you have to sell, isn't it?

Matt's online business is providing those high quality products, so as we have discussed, one lead can create a much greater profit margin with these type of high quality products than one that is being sold low price products. So clearly, you want to work with a company that is offering those high quality products that provide a value-added component for your customers.

Now that you have a better understanding of this as a franchise online opportunity, let's look at why Matt's business is growing so quickly and becoming a company that is making people stand up and take notice.

What makes this online business the Fastest Growing Company in the Industry?

So what has made Matt's online business grow so quickly, while maintaining the quality of the products and the service level? The business continues to be a success because of the people that are making it that way, including those who choose to partner with Matt. This means that they are producing products that are meeting the needs of their customers and their partners. Overtime, they have built a track record of consistency in both how they pay their commissions, how they deliver their products and the value that they offer with every sale. Their staff is knowledgeable, making those customers and franchise partners feel taken care of and confident that their investment was well placed.

When you are looking for an online franchise to invest in, then you need to be looking for the following keys before you make the choice to invest.

1. Are they producing high quality products with value to their customers?
2. What is their reputation like in their specific industry?
3. How are commissions paid? Do you benefit in terms of commissions from follow up sales, or do you only receive commissions from those initial sales? (Remember, it costs more to find those new customers than it does to keep a customer. So is the company passing those cost onto you as their partner?)

4. Do they have a solid training model that walks you through their system step by step?
5. Are their mentors or coaches available to answer any questions that you may have?
6. Can they demonstrate that their system provides long term success rates and solid commission growth over time?

As you can tell, an online business can provide promises of big commissions and no real work, but the reality is that they often are not able to fulfill those promises. The get rich quick scheme is just that, a scheme. There is no business model under the sun that can provide you the ability to earn money without putting out some effort.

If you are looking to do the real work to build a business, then you will need to make sure that business model can support you and help you to grow. Additionally, you want to find mentors who have had their own success with an online business. How did they find success and what types of barriers did they encounter? By taking the time to find a mentor and avail yourself of all the coaching offered by your online franchise company, you can help yourself to grow your business and your income.

Matt offers all of these things and much more to their franchise partners. While they might not be the only internet business out there, they provide one of the most consistent and supportive plans out there. They want their franchise partners to succeed, because when they succeed, Matt's online business is also more successful. If a company is truly looking to grow, they will invest in their franchise partners. Yes, they will really make the effort to invest in you and your business. In the end, you will both benefit from your hard work and willingness to work the program.

If the business model you are looking at doesn't offer support and a solid training program, then they are not poised to help you grow and may not be poised to grow themselves. Matt has provided evidence that their growth is not manufactured, but based on helping their franchisees find their own paths to success with the company. I know that this type of support system isn't found every day, but is worth your serious consideration.

So now that you have a better idea of the type of business opportunity that can be available to you through Matt or any online franchise business. But creating a business takes more than just laying your money down and hoping it would roll back in. It means building a network and creating leads that you can use to grow your customer base. At the same time, it will also mean that you are going to have to work to grow your business, even if you opt for a Done For You franchise business model with an online component. This is where you create positive change in your financial wellbeing in the long term.

Begin With the End in Mind

This section is where I really want to talk about your goals. When you start a project or an online business, you have started it as part of a specific and personal goal that you have made. This could be increasing your income to build a retirement safety net. Or your goal could be to eventually leave your current career and be able to travel or pursue other interests. After all, we only have one life and not many of us want to spend it tied to a desk for 40 to 50 years.

Therefore, before deciding on a business model to invest in and use to start your own business, it is important to outline your goals. You will feel a deeper desire and motivation to take actions that will help you achieve them if you have a made a plan. Included in this plan should be some factors that make you accountable for achieving defined milestones. I am talking about working toward something versus procrastinating and hoping that you will eventually achieve the results that you want.

Here's where working with a mentor or coach can really help. I have provided coaching over the years and I have found that many individuals have goals, but they don't necessarily have a plan to reach those goals. Thus, they are frustrated because they want to achieve something, but they really just don't know how. Here's where coaching and mentoring really come into play. These coaches can help you to define what you want to achieve and also create an actionable plain. When I am coaching various individuals, I am constantly asking them questions. Not only about their goals, but about their lives in general. I try to understand where they are and what is realistic for them to achieve within a given timeframe. Once they achieve that, new goals can be set with a new timeframe. This makes them accountable to themselves and also gives them a game plan.

That end goal can also provide motivation when the going gets tough and they are struggling to meet their milestones on the way to that goal. Additionally, in the face of a setback (and believe me, they do happen!), you can find that end goal is a motivation to get back on your feet after such a setback. Your mindset should be how can I reach my goal, challenging your brain to come up with alternative paths to your end goal. Otherwise, you can create a negative mindset that can build up and actually become a road block to your success overtime. The reality is that you can be your own best tool and ally to building the life you want, or you can be your own worst enemy. The choice is really up to you.

I have shared a lot of information about how to choose an online business and what makes a successful one. Additionally, we have covered how your mindset can impact the success of your business. Now let's look at how continuing your education can really help you to reach these goals.

Chapter 5

Continuing Education - You Can Only Ride One Horse at a Time

No matter what we are doing in our lives, it can be hard to recognize our own limitations. I know that I made decisions that were outside of my range of experience in terms of business multiple times. One of the big decisions I made without the right knowledge was my initial investment with my first business partner. As you remember, I focused more on our friendship and it felt uncomfortable to ask the hard questions that I needed to in order to truly understand the business and what I was investing in.

Another limitation, besides your own knowledge, is that you only have so much time. When it comes to choosing a business model to follow, you have to recognize how much time you really have available to invest in it. When I think about riding one horse at a time, it means recognizing that time limitation in particular. Thus, you may try to find a business model that you can handle around your specific schedule, which includes a full time job or your family obligations.

So what makes any business appealing when you only have a limited amount of time? This is where you might need to consider additional education and training. It can help you to determine which is the best option for you in terms of your time and energy level. You also need to look at what your financial goals are. Is this a business that will take a longer period of time to see a return on your investment or will you start seeing returns fairly early as you work the business?

This is information is key to finding the best match for you in terms of your financial goals. After all, if you are looking to quit a job or retire in the near future, then you might want to look at a Done For You business option with a shorter time frame in terms of return on investment. Translation: you need to spend time educating yourself on the options that are out there. This takes me back to the main point of this chapter, which is that you need to continue to educate yourself on what is going on in the world.

Let's face it, internet business opportunities are the next step in terms of the growth of the internet. As an individual, it seems that I have seen some major technological advancements, including the internet and how it has grown to encompass every facet of our lives. This world wide web that connects our global human family has also given you the ability to shop, express your opinion, find a life partner and even start a business. But before we can dive onto the internet and build a business, we have to understand how individuals are using this medium and how it is impacting their lives.

Continual education means that you are constantly needing to keep yourself open to learn about the ways that people are implementing the internet and other technology in their daily lives. This education can impact your choices in terms of how you decide on what path to take for your internet business. However, continual education needs to go beyond just our financial choices. The reality is that change is occurring constantly in our culture. So the only way to make sure that you are keeping up is to open yourself up to the idea that you need to be willing to keep learning and educating yourself in a variety of areas.

This means taking the time to grow and accept changes in how things are done. One way I can think of is ordering food. There used to be a time when we called the restaurant, placed our order and went to pick up the food. Eventually, delivery became an option if you lived close enough to the restaurant. Now, you can actually place the order online and have it delivered without even talking to a restaurant employee until you meet the delivery person at the door.

Individuals who might be technologically adverse are putting themselves into a position of not being able to take advantage of these options and functions. The point of this example is that if you aren't open to change, you could be missing out on some great opportunities that might really provide you a new way to approach various areas of your life. This isn't just limited to ordering food or other products. It includes new ways to learn about various cultures, business opportunities and even a new way to go to college or university.

Continual education is about more than just making better financial choices. It is also about improving yourself in a variety of areas. This could be more than just finding new ways to reach your goals. It could also mean finding new experiences that can help you grow in terms of how you view the world and the various cultures and societies that are out there.

The world is full of experiences that are just waiting for us to come and take advantage of them. Those individuals who close themselves off from a mindset of continually learning can often find themselves in a position where they do not grow, but instead they stagnate. This stagnation is not limited the financial or professional aspects of their lives, but also the personal. When we stop trying to learn, we stop growing.

So what are some areas that we can use to keep growing and learning? Here are just a few ways that we can continue our life long education. You might be able to think of others, but these are just a few suggestions to get you started.

Take a Class Online or In Person

The internet provides us an opportunity to not only grow our financial income, but we can also use it to expand our knowledge. This also means that even if we don't live in a place that has college or other opportunities for continuing education, we can still take advantage of continuing education through the classes that might be offered through the internet. There are classes on financial management, learning how to use various appliances, how to fix a variety of products or even home improvement projects.

You do not need to even pay money for classes either. YouTube has amassed a huge library of videos on how to do everything from cook to make car repairs. If there is anything you want to learn or explore, there is probably a video on the internet for that with step by step instructions. For a vast majority of the YouTube channels, you can subscribe to a company or individual and watch videos on a variety of topics based on what they have to offer.

The point of this type of education is to expand your horizons, even if you are never going to become a member of the automotive club or be a gourmet chef. Still, the most important thing to remember is that you are trying to grow as an individual. However, don't try to learn how to do several things at one time. It might be overwhelming if you have multiple continual learning opportunities happening at the same time.

That being said, some of us are multi-taskers. The reality is that you might find yourself in a position where you enjoy exploring multiple areas at the same time. Others can find it overwhelming. Essentially, you have to decide what type of individual you are and then begin to explore topics at a speed that works for you.

Certification classes can also be offered through your local school system or even through a community foundation or group. The point is that classes or educational opportunities are available in a variety of settings, but you need to extend yourself to look for them. Even your local library can be a great source of material to continue your education, just by picking up some new reading material or textbooks.

These types of classes are also a great way to start a new hobby. If you are looking for a new experience but not necessary a structured class or instruction manual, there are many opportunities to explore through the internet. This technological wonder can allow you to be introduced to hobbies and opportunities that you might not have even known existed.

Pick Up a New Hobby

It seems that a hobby would hardly fit under the category of continual education, but you would be amazed what you can learn by just picking up a hobby. Take knitting. This is a hobby that allows you to create a variety of items, from a scarf to a large blanket. My mother did it for years. It can be done while you watch television or listen to music. Many individuals talk about how relaxing it can be, plus it is a way to keep your brain active. As you can see, a good hobby can have a variety of benefits for you in terms of your health, emotionally and mentally. But it can also be a great way to deal with change. You had to know that I was coming back to that, right?

Here's how you can use a hobby to help you deal with the stress of change. The first is that a hobby can help you to destress from a traumatic change by taking your mind off of the situation for a period of time. The rhythm of your hobby can help you to relax for a moment. If you are dealing with a change that is positive, your hobby can be a way to celebrate that positive change in your life.

I know individuals who love to fish. They take their time and relax, enjoying nature while they are trying to catch the big one. Fishing also becomes a time to have conversations with loved ones, often that get into very deep topics just by virtue of the quieter setting and time together.

In the time that I have spent coaching (which has become a hobby of mine), I was never so excited and nervous as I was when I started coaching my son. Now I had to step out of the role of being his parent and instead step into a different type of authority figure in his life. While it was an adjustment for him and me, we both made it. The result of this period of time is that our relationship has actually changed for the better. I have noticed that we have drawn closer and been able to discuss a variety of topics. Learning what my son really thinks has been enlightening, but also has helped me to be a better parent. My point is that your hobby can often have unexpected, but pleasant, consequences. Changes for the better and all you have to do is be willing to spend some time enjoying a hobby.

But what if you are not the hobby type? Never really clicked with a particular hobby? Then you can really continue your education by learning what types of hobbies there are available. Let me assure you that there are plenty out there if you are willing to explore. Here are just a few ideas that can get you started in your hobby hunt.

Finding a new hobby can be as simple as checking out the classes available at your local library or community center. Often, they can give you an opportunity to try something out, but with a limited financial investment on your part. Other ways to find a new hobby is asking friends and family what they enjoy. Also, just by trying something new and being willing to explore, you may easily find a variety of hobby ideas. By getting into your community and exploring, you may find that your next hobby is waiting just outside your front door.

Learn by Helping Others

While it might seem out of place in a section about continual learning, volunteering is a great way to help you to grow and learn something new. With my coaching, not only did it help me to reach out to help the young men and their families in my community, I found it to be a great way to step outside of my life's stresses and focus on others. You would be amazed at how much getting to know others and what they are struggling with can help you to gain some perspective on the changes in your own life.

With a new perspective, we might find that what changes we are dealing with are not so bad and that they might even be manageable. At the same time, helping others can also give us a new viewpoint of our own ability to adapt to change. We might find that we are more open to learning from the change, instead of just focusing on the negative aspects and how they are going to impact us personally.

Getting out with others can also help us to get out of our own head for a while. This means we aren't focusing on our own life, but focusing outside of ourselves. It can be amazing what those periods of time can do for our wellbeing mentally, but also physically, as you will see later.

Explore Nature

Hiking or other physical activities can help us to look outside of ourselves in terms of the world at large. We can learn more about ourselves as we contemplate the physical world around us. Look at the amazing opportunities to explore and enjoy new experiences in our national or local parks. Of course, this is just one example. There are so many other ways to get active and learn more about how our world works.

Nature can also provide us a way to relax in a setting far away from the hustle and bustle of our technological world. This quiet time can help us to examine our lives and our own beliefs. In the quiet of nature, away from the hustle and bustle of urban living, we can visualize what change looks like in our own lives. It can also be a great time to build our own set of goals, determining what we want from our lives based on the quiet time with our thoughts or a through a spirited discussion with a close friend on a hike or boating activity. I enjoy sports, as evident by my coaching. But regardless, I find that my kids, especially my son, are more willing to open up about their lives and experiences when they share in a physical activity with you.

Throughout any of these activities, you will find that your viewpoint on life is changed. I encourage you to embrace that changing viewpoint. It can lead you to embrace other changes in your life with a more positive outlook. Why is our outlook on change so important? Simply put, because of the nature of change itself.

Changes are happening all around us, whether we want them to or not. Our children are getting older and so are our parents. People we thought would be in our lives forever move on and disappear. Technology continues to top itself with every new version of the smartphone or latest app. Even politics and the global community are constantly changing to meet the needs of their people. Cultures have shifts as ideals are challenged, struck down and replaced.

Trauma and natural disasters happen in all our lives. Investments suffer losses and our families struggle through hard times. But we also have changes that can make profound impacts on us in a positive way. However, no matter what the change, we need to be focused on how to make the most of it. Every change is a chance to learn and grow if we approach it the right way. Embracing change means being willing to accept that it is always happening, but that it doesn't have to necessarily be a negative occurrence. In fact, it can be a chance to continue our own personal education. Build upon these experiences and use them to help yourself grow as a human being.

Traumatic change can also have an impact on our mindset and overall way of thinking. As we will discuss in the next chapter, our mindset can have a large impact on how we view change. In cases of trauma, it might be a case of expanding our own horizons, even gaining a deeper spiritual perspective as a result. Does that mean we do not have to acknowledge the negative impacts of the change? Of course you should, but you should not let the negative aspects overwhelm you. Our whole chapter has been about continuing education and how we can use it to grow in the face of change. So even traumatic changes can be opportunities to learn and grow. But what makes growth so key?

Growth is another important part of embracing change. Every change can provide us an opportunity to grow and thrive or to shrink back and make no adjustments in our lives. An often heard quote attributed to Albert Einstein is, "The definition of insanity is doing the same thing over and over, expecting different results."

So it is with change. Are we approaching it the same way over and over again, but expecting different results? Our continuing education allows us to approach change from a different perspective each time, therefore we can see different results and benefits from every change in our lives. At the same time, continuing education means that we are approaching change differently, learning even from our failures. As an individual, we are thus growing and making our lives fuller, mostly because we are willing to embrace change, instead of looking at it fearfully.

Therefore, we aren't doing things exactly the same, but we are continuing to do things differently, making adjustments throughout our lives. Change requires us to be ready to adjust and education that encourages growth means that we are ready when life throws changes at us.

Still, as I mentioned, your mindset is a key part of how you deal with change and how you approach and internalize the results. It can also have an impact on how you choose to act in the face of change. Now it is time to explore our mindset and its overall impact.

Chapter 6

Hopes and Dreams for the Future

No matter how much we try to avoid the bad in life, it is inevitably going to happen to us at some point. There has never been someone in the world who has not had to deal with various challenges and pressures, as well as the results of positive and negative changes. The reality is that since we will all face these issues at some point, we need to find a way to deal with them. One of the first ways is deciding on our mindset in advance.

Are You Positive or Negative?

Our mindset is often a reflection of how we tend to view our lives in general. If we tend to view the different aspects of our lives in a negative fashion, our mindset will eventually become very negative. The reality is that this will then make change more difficult for us to deal with and also have a negative impact on a variety of areas of our lives. How could that be?

First, negative thinking and a negative mindset will often place us in the position of viewing change as a bad thing. We are often stuck in a routine, because as individuals, we may not like the idea of exploring new things or chasing new experiences. Additionally, when we start looking at our financial opportunities, we tend to be less likely to take a risk in terms of investments, because we can only see what could go wrong instead of what could go right.

But there is a physical impact to a negative mindset. We tend to place our bodies into a negative stress mode more frequently. This mode can be a strain on our hearts, lungs, blood pressure and multiple organs. Overtime, we find our bodies simply cannot keep up with the stress mode any longer and it translates into poor health. Suddenly we are now dealing with another change in terms of medications and potentially chronic conditions, which impact our ability to enrich our lives. Instead, we find ourselves even more limited and of course, more stressed out. So the cycle continues and our bodies continue to show wear and tear as a result.

Our negative viewpoint can make this situation even worse, because we tend to dwell on it and our brain makes the situation seem even more negative than it was to start with. Dwelling on it, therefore, ends up compounding the problem in the long run. Here are just a few of the other aspects that you have to consider when it comes to negative thinking. Keep a look out for the negative cycles that can develop with each of these as we discuss them.

Feeling down – Negative thinking can lead to negative feelings, which include anger, frustration, irritability, anxiety and even depression. However, you can deal with a lot of other feelings, but this is never a pleasant place to be and it can make it hard for you to really enjoy all the various aspects of your life. Plus, once you start feeling down, it can be really hard to pull yourself out of a cycle of focusing on why you are feeling that way. Overtime, your negative thoughts and mindset can make feeling down or seeing the worst in people and circumstances your way of life.

Physical effects – We have talked about the negative impact physically, but here are just a few more of those potential physical effects to consider. The body lowers its defenses, because negative thinking has a negative impact on your energy levels and your body's immune system. Why do you think individuals who suffer with depression always mention how tired they feel and tend to be sick more often? We can also have a negative impact on how we care for ourselves, such as eating properly and getting enough sleep. This can lead to our being more susceptible to disease, because our body is not in optimal shape to fight it off. There are a variety of other physical issues negative thinking can bring in our lives, but you get the point. Negative thinking is more than a mental problem; it also has real physical consequences that can often lead to negative consequences that compound our negative thinking. It becomes a vicious cycle.

Close off the possibilities – When it comes to dealing with change, if we have a negative attitude or mindset, the possibilities that come from the change could be totally missed. Simply put, our negative state tends to push off those elements that would make us excited about change. Instead, we tend to attract circumstances that support us in thinking something is always wrong about change, and so we get stuck. Suddenly, we are creating a negative life, which just supports our negative thinking. Again, see the cycle?

Negative impact on others – Our negative thinking can often showcase in how we speak with others. If we are always complaining or seeing the worst of every situation, then we can bring down those around us. After a period of time, we might find that there are less individuals who want to spend time around our negative outlook. This leads to isolation, which can only compound our negative thinking. Another cycle in the making.

Secondly, when we are complaining about a change and focused on the negative, it makes it hard or next to impossible for us to find solutions to the challenges that the change presents. If others present an idea to you, your negative mindset looks for reasons why their idea won't work versus how it can actually have a positive impact on your situation. At the same time, we also won't be focusing on the opportunities that a change might be presenting for ourselves and our families. Really, a negative point of view or mindset can have a broad impact over our whole life, but definitely not a positive one.

As I went through my divorce, I wasn't necessarily focused on how it could end up having a positive impact on my life. At first, it was hard to see how ending one relationship was opening the door for a better long term relationship with my new wife. But that was exactly what was happening. Overtime, particularly as I kept my journal of that time period, I can see how my thinking was negative, but gradually, I could see how traveling and exploring helped to brighten my mindset. It didn't happen overnight and changing your mindset can take some time as well. But you can do it! But let's talk about why negative thinking seems to be our default mindset, particularly in times of change.

What makes us default to a negative pattern of thought? Negative thoughts are often caused by ingrained thinking patterns as they relate to our own beliefs. Essentially, when we make a habit of thinking about our life experiences negatively, then we are reinforcing our negative belief system. Later on, every situation will seem to prove us right in terms of thinking the worst. It essentially becomes a self-fulfilling prophecy. This type of thinking pattern can start when we are a child and continue into adulthood.

The reality is that we build a belief system over the course of our lives. Some of that belief system is based on information taught to us by our parents, extended families, educational systems, religious training and cultural influences. Yet that only builds a foundation and then we add to our beliefs based on our own experiences.

Take the time to examine your beliefs. Are they still serving you or could they be limiting your ability to embrace change and move forward? Are your beliefs stopping you from embracing a risk or trying a new experience? If so, that belief may need to be changed, thus allowing you to embrace all that life has to offer.

Self-knowledge and understanding take time to build, but the rewards can include a better way to embrace changes in our lives, both personal or professional. Let's look at some of the ways that positive thinking can impact our lives, but in a way that we will appreciate much more.

Life Happens, So Embrace It

We are going to discuss a few ways that positive thinking can have an impact on our lives. As I talked about with a negative mindset, there is more going on than just thoughts in our heads. First of all, we want to be clear that positive thinking involves more than just an upbeat attitude or being happy. While it might have not necessarily been thought of as a term on the same level as persistence or work ethic, this line of thought has changed over the years.

Research has begun to show that positive thinking is about creating real value in your life and building a skill set that can help you cope with the ups and downs of life. As with negative thinking, positive thinking has the ability to impact your health, work and personal life. Negative thoughts tend to narrow our mind down to just one or two possibilities, and focusing us only those possibilities. Thus, your options are limited and in some ways, negative thinking allows you to shut out the world around you.

But when we experience positive thoughts and emotions, our brains also expand to include more possibilities and our minds are thus more open to exploring options when it comes to dealing with a variety of situations.

However, there are more benefits in terms of positive thinking. One such benefit is that by being open to more possibilities, we are more open to learning and enhancing our skill sets, as well as developing resources for use in our lives. These resources can be helpful in a variety of situations, both now and in the future. The best part of these skills and resources is that they will often stick with us longer than the emotions that allowed us to develop them in the first place. As you can see, positive thoughts and emotions can have a long term effect long after the initial moment where those feelings or thoughts occurred.

Additionally, positive thinking can also help us to reduce stress, which can have a positive impact on our overall health. Positive thinkers can see a few of the following physical benefits:

- Increased life span
- Lower rates of depression
- Lower levels of distress
- Greater resistance to the common cold

- Better psychological well-being
- Reduced risk of death from a cardiovascular disease or event
- Better overall coping skills, particularly during times of stressful change

In addition, you find that you have the ability to bring peace into your life during times of difficulty and also the ability to make greater connections with others. So why do receive these benefits from positive thinking?

These benefits appear to occur in part because when you are better able to deal with stress, you reduce the effects of stress on your body overall. Positive thinkers tend to also be healthier overall, because they seem to engage in a healthier lifestyle consistently in terms of a healthier diet and more physical activity.

To better understand how positive thinking can be so powerful, we need to think in terms of our self-talk. After all, we all talk to ourselves. This is really the internal dialogue that we have with ourselves to justify a particular choice or determine if a course of action is the right one to take. This could include mentally walking through the potential consequences of our choices before we make them. Self-talk really includes that endless stream of unspoken thoughts that we have on a daily basis. Some of it comes from logic and reason, but also can be built on misconceptions that you create because of a lack of information about the situation.

When we talked about internal dialogue in the section on negative thinking, we discuss how we can create a repeating internal dialogue of negative self-talk. The same can be done with positive self-talk. Change often brings challenges. Our self-talk, if it is positive, can help us to embrace those challenges. Simply put, it will help us to use the challenges to build skills and resources. Notice that we can translate that into growth!

We have discussed how change can help us to grow, but it is also clear that our ability to use positive self-talk can also do the same thing. Not only that, but if we are determined to practice positive thinking, we can find that we are more likely to capitalize on all the good things that happen in our lives. No matter what comes our way, we are more inclined to take advantage of these opportunities, instead of shutting ourselves off from them.

So what are some methods to help you make the transition from a negative self-talk to a more positive one? I have put a few of them below, but these are just to get you started. As you explore new opportunities, you may find other things that help you to maintain your positive self-talk.

Meditation – Research has shown that individuals who practice meditation on a daily basis are able to display more positive emotions than those that do not make a practice of meditation on a daily basis. People who meditate also tend to build valuable skill sets that are still with them in the long term. The benefits don't end either or plateau, but they continue to display increased mindfulness, a greater purpose in life, increased social support and decreased incidents of illness.

If you have never meditated before and are looking for a simple way to start, there are multiple books on meditation. However, you can simply find a time each day when you sit quietly, explore a specific topic in your mind without any distractions. There are potentially spiritual components that you can choose to add, but those are not necessary. Essentially, you are taking time for yourself, allowing time for reflection and quiet thought. This can often help to bring a sense of pause when our lives are particularly chaotic.

In the world we live in, I know that we are always connected to our jobs and our loved ones through technology. Sometimes it can often feel as if we are glued to our phones. But the reality is that by taking a few moments each day to disconnect from our phones and technology, we can actually be embracing a way of life that will give us the foundation to accept and embrace all the changes that come our way.

Writing – Taking the time to write about a positive experience on a daily basis can improve our mood, result in better overall health and less illnesses. The reason is that we are focusing on what is going well versus focusing on what is going wrong. It can also make you focus on what is making you feel more upbeat. When I was dealing with my divorce, I found that I was journaling or writing about my feelings throughout the day, helped me because I was expressing what was going on in my head. This meant that I wasn't dwelling on it constantly either.

I have to say that writing can really be a way for you to get out of your own head and instead focus on what you can learn from the situation versus the details of the situation itself. However, once you write about your feelings or experiences, it is important to look for the positive versus the negative to really see the benefits in the short term, as well as the long run.

Getting into a writing schedule is all about creating a routine. This means that you need set a time aside for writing and make sure that you keep to that schedule. Overtime, you will become so accustomed to doing it that your writing will become second nature to you. I have been using my appointment books as a journal of sorts throughout the years. With stacks of books, I can look through and see the small, as well as large, changes that I have experienced.

Play – Schedule time to play in the course of your life. Is your life scheduled full of meetings, work, responsibilities and appointments? It is clear that we tend to schedule ourselves to the point that we don't have any real downtime. Yet if we don't take the time to stop and appreciate our lives, we can find ourselves struggling to deal with change and maintain our positive outlook on life.

On the other hand, when we take the time to stop and enjoy the flowers, it is amazing what it can do for our state of mind. Play can be any new adventure, but the point is to keep taking time to actually live your life. Doing so will contribute to your happiness and overall contentment of your life. After all, what is the point of working so hard if we don't take the time to smile and enjoy those positive emotions in our lives?

When I took that time to travel after my divorce, I found myself able to step outside of what was going on in my personal life and focus on the world around me. Traveling was a form of healing, but it also helped me to face the challenge of moving on with my life because I was experiencing life. Joy can be found in learning new things, but it can also be found in exploring the world at large, seeing new places, meeting new people. Learn how to let go and have fun, be happy!

A point for us all to keep in mind, researchers have noticed, a compounding effect that occurs with happy people. If they are happy, they develop new skills, which lead to new success and that contributes to their happiness. It's a happiness cycle and one you would appreciate having made the effort to get onto. Well that's great when things are going well and changes are positive ones. But what happens when changes are just hard challenges that drain us of our resources? I will explore that next.

Never Quit

Positive thinking and creating a positive mindset means that we are going to be in a better position to address the challenges in our lives that come as part of change. I know that every change does not appear wonderful at first. Some changes are just plain hard. They can include challenges that almost seem too much in terms of what we can handle.

Failures are also changes that we have to deal with. Financially, we can fail in terms of a new investment or chosen the wrong type of rental property to purchase. When we have those moments of failure, it can be frustrating to us both mentally and emotionally. During those times, it can be difficult to maintain our positive thinking and mindset.

When my business investment failed, I struggled to not only figure out what went wrong, but with the financial loss as well. It was harder to make the decision to invest again, because I now had an experience of being burned. Yet, in order to really move forward, I had to be willing to pick myself up and try again.

The reality is that you will have more failures throughout your life. They will not always be associated with pleasant experiences or changes. In fact, they can be rather painful at times. Losing a home or living through a natural disaster can often seem like a change that you cannot recover from. But the reality is that you can and you will.

I have continued to point to your mindset throughout this book. The reality is that without a positive mindset, you cannot learn from the failures and those circumstances that knock you down. If you aren't willing to learn from those experiences, you cannot really grow and prepare yourself to face the next challenge.

Do you want to move in the direction of what you want to achieve in your life? Then you need to be willing to expend the time and energy to learn from your failures. Thinking positively can give you the courage to tackle change, even when it comes initially wrapped in failure. In fact, you can start to see failure as exciting, because it means that you can get the opportunity to try again. You begin to see what is possible, instead of just focusing on what didn't go right.

The key here is to be persistent. Pick yourself up from failure and move forward, determined to succeed. Learn from what went wrong, make corrections and try again. There is so much out there to learn and explore. Change prompts us to do so, but if we mire ourselves in negative thinking, we aren't going to take advantage of all that change has to offer. Lean on your mentors and personal support team to help you when needed.

Another important point is that you also need to be willing to say no. In personal relationships, it means saying no to overcommitting yourself. In your financial decisions, it means saying no, even to a friend if the numbers don't make sense. Positive thinking doesn't negate making logical decisions. But it does mean that we can courageously make them and move forward with our lives.

I have written a lot about how to embrace change, how to get the right mindset for change and how learning can help you to get the best from every change in your life. Now I want to move forward and discuss some opportunities where you could work with me in a coaching opportunity. This can help you to grow financially, but also continue learning about the world around you. So let's dive into the opportunities that you can take advantage of.

Chapter 7

Move Forward With Me

Over the course of this chapter, I am going to discuss some areas where you can choose to make some major changes in your lives. Some relate to your finances, but others can relate to various areas in your life where you want to make significant changes. We have discussed how your mindset is key to making change work for you and also allow you to embrace it effectively.

Yet I don't just talk about change, I'm willing to work with you and help you to create change in your life. Below are just a few of the areas that I can work with you to help create the change that you want to see in your life. Let's face it, financial change usually allows us to make significant changes in other areas of our lives. With improvement to our finances, we are now in the position to make different choices about how we live and work.

So let's talk about ways to make that financial change and then we will talk about how you can make other changes in your life. Throughout this chapter, I'll discuss how I can help you to make the most out of your life by embracing change.

Real Estate – Partner with Me

When it comes to investing, real estate has always been one of those investments that seemed to be a no brainer. It was always going to make money has been the myth. Yet, that isn't always the case. The reality is that if you aren't careful, real estate can end up being very costly. If you don't make smart choices, then you will find that you have real estate that isn't making you money, but actually costing you money and eating into your financial nest egg. What are some of the ways that you can lose?

1. **Overpay for Your Real Estate**
   Choosing real estate to purchase for an investment is all about the numbers. As much as you love a house, you aren't going to be living there. So you need to determine how much the house costs and what will be your carrying costs each month. Carrying costs are the cost of the mortgage, insurance and property taxes. In addition, if the house does not have a renter, then you need to factor in the costs of having the utilities on, such as water, gas and electric. If you are doing renovations, it is important to make sure that you aren't over improving your real estate for the neighborhood.
   Why is this important? Because if you have a house that is over improved, you won't be able to sell it for what you paid for it. As a result, you are not building equity, which is key to building your net worth in real estate. At the same time, you are not likely to get the rent price that you would need to cover your expenses for the improvements and your monthly overhead.

2. **Not Building Equity**

   If you are making improvements to the real estate you purchase, you need to make sure that you are buying it at a low enough price that your improvements will be able to improve the value of the home. This means that you will be building equity. If you are choosing to be a landlord, then you will find that you are building wealth in two ways. One, you are getting a rent check every month. Your monthly rent needs to be enough to cover the carrying costs and allow you to put some away for maintenance issues down the line. If after all that, you have some profit, then you are definitely on the right track. Yet, even if you are just covering the expenses of the property with the rent, you are also paying down the mortgage and building equity. When you sell the house, you will be able to see that profit in terms of being able to tap that equity as part of the transfer of the property.

3. **Not Doing Your Due Diligence on Your Renters**

   While it might seem easy to find renters for your property, finding quality renters is not that easy. When you get those renters that are not quality, it ends up costing you money in terms of repairs and legal costs. So it is critical that you do your background checks, looking for instances where they didn't pay their rent or they were evicted. This can be a clue that they might be a potentially problem renter.

   What if you have a renter that passes your background check, but turns out to be a non-paying or destructive tenant? Then you need to make sure that you are familiar with the tenant laws in your state. Every state or locality is different, so it is critical to know what your rights and responsibilities are before you even sign your first lease. After all, you may be forced to have a non-paying tenant on your property throughout the eviction process, which could be months. This will be a costly outlay, in terms of your out-of-pocket costs to cover the monthly overhead of the property while you are completing the legal process.

4. **Not Properly Maintaining Your Property**
    This one might seem like a no-brainer, but the reality is that many landlords choose to do minimal upgrades, but not the routine maintenance. Overtime, a neglected property can stop making money, because renters won't stay or worse yet, they sue because of issues with the property. Either way, maintaining the property can keep you in a much better financial situation in the long run.

    Therefore, you want to set up a maintenance schedule and be sure to notify your tenants. Most laws require that you give your tenants notice before you are coming to inspect or complete routine maintenance on the property. So be sure that you know those rules and always notify your tenants in a timely manner. By keeping up with the maintenance, you can reduce your overhead in the long run.

As you can see, there is plenty involved in terms of being a landlord, but also in making sure that your properties are a financially sound investment. I would love to work with you to help you take the next step into your financial future by mentoring you through the purchase of your first property. This is an investment that can continue to grow as time goes by and is worth taking the time to learn how to do it right.

I can help you learn from my mistakes, so that you can create an impactful change in your finances right from your first property onward. Now let's discuss another area where I would welcome the opportunity to partner with you!

Money on the Internet

The Internet has become a booming source of income in the last decade. Individuals who once were limited to the stores and retail opportunities in their area, they are now able to shop in a global marketplace. With the various opportunities available, it can be easy to see why you might get confused or even discouraged at the possibility of finding the right opportunity for you and your family. After all, you might not have a lot to invest, but you still want to find a way to make that investment grow. The reality is that banks aren't offering much in the way of interest on money sitting in a savings account. Therefore, you need to find a way to make your money work for you, providing income now and into the future.

As we discussed earlier, there are plenty of franchise opportunities available on the internet. However, there are also plenty of scams. The reality is that you need to be cautious when choosing an internet business opportunity to invest in. Therefore, it is important to do your homework. What type of time commitment do you want to make to a new business? If you aren't able to devote a large amount of time, it would be best to consider business opportunities that will allow you to enjoy a Done For You business program.

These types of programs allow you to just plug in and follow a plan to build your business. Depending on the business, you may actually end up being an affiliate. This means that you are sending leads to the larger companies by distributing ads or other information and providing a link to your specific landing page. By using and developing your own network, you are able to start to build your business.

The beauty of being an affiliate is that you are going to be able to enjoy all the support of the larger company, but not the costs of carrying inventory or employees. Therefore, you have the beauty of owning your own business, but not all the overhead that would be involved in a traditional business.

Having been an employee and a partner in a business that includes employees, I understand what is involved when it comes to creating and building a business. I too have looked at the internet for income streams. Working with you, I can help you to pinpoint the right internet business for you and your circumstances. Plus, I can give you the benefits of my own research and business experience to help you make the right change in this area of your life. Of course, working with you, I can also point you to business opportunities that are truly Done For You programs, which make it easier for you to get started, even if you aren't as familiar with the technology of the internet. However, my experiences with change mean that I have experience in a variety of areas, including investing in an established business. Let's explore the opportunities that could be available to you.

Invest in a Business

Financial investments can be a great opportunity for you to grow your net worth, allowing your investment to make money for you while you work on other opportunities. So the question is what should you be aware of before you invest as a silent or minority partner in a business? Here are a few points to keep in mind.

1. **Ask for the financials** – The reality is that a business owner looking to take on a partner is in need of capital. The question you want to know is why? Looking at their financials, you can see if the business is bleeding funds or if they are in fact making the types of sales that would be considered key to growing the business. If they are hesitant to let you see the financials of the business, this should be a potential red flag.

   Once you look at the financials, you need to make sure that you are asking questions about their monthly sales, the monthly expenses and how much profit they are making on a monthly basis. When you are considering making an investment into a business, it is important to understand how the business is operating financially and if it can meet necessary obligations. If it is a struggling business, you may find that your investment goes out the window.

2. **Know your role** – With a partnership, there are a variety of roles that you can take. You could be a silent partner with no role in the day to day operations. This also means that you might have little say in the choices that your partner is making in the business. On the other hand, if you are going to be a more active partner, then you may have more of a role in how the business is operating. No matter what your role, you want to make sure that you define a plan where you can step in if the business is being run into the ground, so that you can protect your investment.

Many partnerships have a contract that defines roles and what are the scenarios that would allow the partnership to be dissolved. Make sure that you have reviewed that partnership agreement, preferably with an attorney. This way you won't be surprised later if any of those clauses come into play.

3. **Put it in writing** – While this might seem like a given, there are many partnerships built on a handshake and a verbal agreement. The problem is that when the partnership struggles or there are disagreements between the partners, the business suffers as a result. Without a clear path in writing, either partner could make decisions that directly impact the business without consulting the other. Therefore, you want to be sure that you have a written and executed document that you could take to court if necessary to enforce your rights as a minority or silent partner.

4. **Learn about the industry** – If you are not familiar with the industry, then it is important to do your homework. Don't just trust on your partner to fill you in on what you need to know. Note that continuing education is coming up again. Making an investment means understanding the industry and the product that you are investing in. Here's the reality: your new partner could claim that this is a growing industry, but it could actually be shrinking. Therefore, doing your due diligence can include talking with current customers, industry professionals and experts. The idea is to understand what can be defined as growth in that industry.

For example, are they seeing a steady growth of 5% a year, when the industry is seeing growth at 20%? This could indicate problems with the business model or structure. On the other hand, you might also be able to see that based on industry growth, your investment's rate of return might not be as high as you initially anticipated. Whatever the case, the more you know about the industry, the more informed decision you can make.

5. **Have an exit strategy** – The reality is that businesses grow and change. You might invest with the idea of being involved in the business for a specific period of time. Once that time is done, you want to know how you will be leaving the business. Will someone need to buy you out? Once your initial investment and a defined return amount is paid, will you be relinquishing your partnership role back to the original owner? There are multiple scenarios that could be in play here, so you need to make sure that you and your partner have defined an appropriate exit strategy based on your role in the business.

   Additionally, if you are going to stay with the business during a period of growth, then you need to define the numbers that would signal your time to be bought out.

6. **Understand the economics** – When you are considering investing in a business, you need to make sure that you know how much it costs to create each unit. This is key because if you are losing money on each unit, they are not going to be able to pay their investors. In the long run, it will end up costing you money. The easiest formula to determine per unit cost is to take revenue minus full costs, including marketing and distribution costs. If each unit sells for $2, but takes $2.25 to make, then the business might not be worth investing in.

As you can see, there is plenty to consider when you are making the decision to invest in a business. I have learned a lot since my first partnership and today I have successfully invested in an HVAC business. I asked the hard questions this time and now I have a sound investment. Are you interested investing in a particular business? Let's partner up and I can show you the best methods to reach your financial goals through investing in various businesses, including online ones. Yet I can also provide you the benefits of my skills and experiences in the form of coaching, as I will discuss next.

Coached on Change

As we have discussed, change can happen at any time. To completely embrace a change, we might need input from an individual who is not necessary involved in the situation. The beauty of a third party individual is you can take advantage of a viewpoint from someone who is not invested emotionally or financially in the current situation. In many ways, that viewpoint can be key in showing you another way to approach a situation.

However, coaching can also be key when it comes to motivating change in our lives. Let's face it, as individuals we can find it hard to make a dramatic change without some type of motivation. Life coaches are becoming popular for just that reason. Not only can they help us to deal with change, but they can assist us to create a plan for our lives that allows us to be the ones to create change in our own lives.

So what are some areas of our lives that we might consider using a coach? One big change where a coach can be helpful is when we are navigating the world of a major personal life change. We might be dealing with the ending of a relationship, such as a marriage, and wondering what to do now. How do we embrace the change and create a new course for our lives? In this case, we are not only processing a change, but trying to implement one of our own. A coach can help us to chart a path, giving us goals, assistance in dealing with challenges and obstacles, but also they give us someone to be accountable to. When we are trying to make a change or reach a goal, it can be hard to stay motivated. This is especially true because we can make excuses to ourselves and eventually, we are so off track that we just give up. Think about your New Year's resolutions and how often you have managed to successfully achieve them. If your answer is like most of us, your success rate is less than stellar. This is because in large part, you do not have someone to whom you are accountable.

Additionally, when we do fail or fall off the wagon, we don't reset but just figure that we couldn't do it. This is when we generally give up on that resolution. Using a coach, now we are accountable to someone. But a coach can also help us to reset if we aren't successful right away. Making a change in a habit or way of doing things takes more than just willpower. If that was the case, then everyone who struggles with smoking would be able to quit on their first try. But the reality is that willpower is not enough. Instead, we need a support system.

How many times have we been able to succeed at something with the help of a support system? There are examples from weight loss to dealing with an addiction where a support team can help you to be successful. The point is that using a coach can help you gain the skills you need to achieve your short term goals, but set you up to reach long term goals as well.

Change in your life that you are initiating also needs a support system to be successful. A coach can be that support team. This means they can help you get back up after a failure, but also help you to make adjustments to avoid that kind of failure again. At the same time, a coach can help you set up your goals and a road map to reach them.

Now keep in mind, a coach is not the same as a mentor. As I pointed out earlier, a mentor will be part of a long term relationship and work with you in a variety of areas of your life. On the other hand, as a coach, I can help you to tackle a specific change in your life. The benefit is that by the time we are done, you will have a new set of skills to fall back on in terms of the next big change in your life.

I love working with others and helping them to learn how to embrace change for its positive impacts. The best part about change is how it can be a force for personal and professional growth. No matter what you hope to accomplish, I am willing to help you grow your skill set on coping with and thriving from change!

Build a Custom Home – Mistakes to Avoid

Finally, I want to discuss custom home building. Remember in chapter 2, I discussed this as one of the failures that I learned from. The reality is that I love the idea of building custom homes to meet the needs of my clients. I love see their faces when we get the design right and the perfect layout for their family. If you are interested in building your own custom home, I can help you to get started, but also let you know about the potential mistakes you could make that would cost you money.

Here are just a few of the top ones, but there are plenty of areas that you need to consider when building a home. By avoiding these areas, you can make your building experience one that you will look back on as a positive experience. Working with me, I can help you to spot any potential mistakes and build your own skill level in this area to create the home of your dreams.

1. **Acting as Your Own General Contractor**

   When you act as your own general contractor, the reality is that you do not know what you do not know. While it might seem to be a place to save money on your build, you will find that you do not have all the skill sets needed to get the job done on time and on budget.

   For example, a general contractor has relationships that they have built overtime with subcontractors, including roofers, plumbers and electricians. While you might not think that you need that relationship, after all you won't be hiring them again, but they depend on repeat business. Essentially, if you need them to meet a tight timeframe, they aren't likely to be as quick to meet your need as they would if it was a general contractor that they work for regularly. Then your schedule will suffer as they put your work after their regular contractors. When one sub doesn't show, then you will find that it has a direct impact on the rest of the subs and the time frame of your home build.

   Another way that a general contractor can be beneficial is that they will make sure that the subs are completing the work correctly and using the right materials. As much as you want to believe in everyone's honesty, the reality is that subs can be known to cut corners, especially when dealing with home owners that don't know any better. This is a recipe for disaster, especially later when you are having problems with your home.

Additionally, you can save money with a general contractor, because he can keep the costs of the subs down. How? Because of his relationship and the fact that they want to keep working with him will make them able to negotiate the pricing. In the end, a general contractor can provide a skill set that you are completely lacking, which makes it worth having one.

2. **Get and Use a Quality Set of Plans**

The reality is that without a good set of plans, you are going to make mistakes. Those mistakes are going to end up costing you money in the run. Here are just a few of those ways. One, you can't get accurate cost estimates for materials and labor without a set of plans. You also can't make an accurate materials list, so your contractor would not be able to order things in a timely fashion. Being able to make a budget for your house is key before you even start building your home, because your budget will help you decide where you want to be spending money in terms of materials and finishes, so that you can make the right choices for your circumstances.

Plans also are the instruction manual for your subs. Without them, it can get expensive as your subs complete work but then have to make changes due to misunderstandings, expensive tear-outs, delays and conflicts between your subs, each of which has their own opinions. Marks and notes could be interpreted differently by each of your subs, especially if the plans are not clear, but marked with plenty of pencil notes.

To get the best discount in terms of materials, you want to be able to order all at once. When you are ordering piecemeal or to cover a tear-out, you aren't taking advantage of that discount. The result is that you are spending additional money that you weren't expecting to. Not to mention the costs in terms of delays. Remember, your subs will move to the next project if you aren't ready for them, so every delay is costing you time and money.

At the same time, you need to make sure that the plans fit your lot. After all, it won't work if your lot doesn't have the right slope for a walkout basement, but your plans call for one. That could end up costing a lot of money in terms of grading and adjustments to your foundation.

3. Choose the Right General Contractor

I have convinced you that you need a general contractor, if for no other reason that you need to keep your house on budget and on time. Yet, if you choose the wrong general contractor, you are still going to end up paying for it and the cost can be high. So get referrals and check them out. Do you know someone who had work done by that general contractor? What was their experience? Check out a couple of jobs in progress. Are they neat or does it look like they aren't keeping up with the trash and excess materials? Look at the work. Is it fitting together or do you see warped boards? Remember a good general contractor will take pride in their work and that will show on their job sites.

Check references but also ask the references if they know anyone else who has worked with this contractor and get in contact with them if possible. Also, ask about the subcontractors and talk with them. The point is to determine that they are going to meet your standards, plus you can get to know how they interact with the general contractor. You should consider getting references from the subs as well and check them out.

4. **Foundation is Key**

   When it comes to your home, you need to make sure that you have the foundation completed correctly. This means holding your concrete sub accountable for making sure the concrete is completed correctly. If it isn't level, then nothing else in your house can be either. So you want to make sure that concrete is the right grade and strength for your particular house plan and lot. Additionally, you need to make sure that the piers and supports are put in the right places to avoid settling and cracks in your walls and home.

   The point is that you need to make sure that your contractor is up to speed on your plans and that they are making the right adjustments to the concrete to build a solid foundation. Yet, you have to remember that this principle can apply throughout your custom home. Ask questions and make sure that you are doing your research. See how that ties back to my points about continuing education?

5. **Engineered Products as Building Materials**

   When you take advantage of engineered products, you are building a home with a product designed for that specific project. For example, if you use a roof truss system, then you can be sure that the weight of the roof will fall in the right place on the load bearing walls and beams. When it is built by the general contractor, you run the risk that the weight of the roof is transferred to walls that weren't meant to be load bearing.

Engineered products can be more effective in terms of being designed specifically for your home and they will perform as expected. Plus, they typically are easier to install and can save you money in the long run. It's a good option to consider from your floors to your roof. But you need to do your homework to find the right engineered products for your home based on your specific plans. Plus, there are a variety of products out there, so you want to make sure that you have really compared and contrasted based on what you need for your home. Plus, you need to compare apples to apples in terms of the product's warranty and the overall lifetime of the product.

6. **Build to Your Needs**

When it comes to deciding on the plans for your house, it can be an exciting process. You might be tempted to build in all your dreams, but that might not be realistic for your budget. So you need to remember to design around your needs and any anticipated needs of your family. If this is meant to be a retirement home, then designing for potential wheelchair use in the future or other concerns would be worth it.

If you need more square footage than the budget allows, consider lowering the budget on your finishes in the interior to make up the difference. The reason is that these finishes can be upgraded later as your budget will allow and they will typically need to be replaced anyway. Adding square footage is unfortunately much harder to do in the future.

As you can see, there are a lot of potential mistakes you can make when you start to build a custom home. Working with me, you can not only avoid these mistakes, but many others as well. My experience in this area can be a coaching opportunity for you before you even start your custom home.

Throughout this chapter, I have demonstrated several areas where I would be willing to work with you as a partner or coach. This would allow you to take advantage of my experiences and let you learn from not only my failures, but also my successes.

Change happens to us all, but the type of change I am talking about now is the change that you initiate yourself. Action that will propel you to the next level of your life. But taking those actions require more than just motivation from you, but knowledge and a plan. I can help you to create that plan, but no matter what, you will need to provide the action.

There are so many places in your life where you can embrace change. The point is that you need to embrace change. It is always occurring, but with a positive mindset, it can be a source of growth and opportunity throughout your life!

Conclusion

Throughout this book, not only have I focused on change and how we can deal with it, but also on how to make changes that can have a positive impact on your life. Personally, I believe in coaching and making a difference in the lives of others. So what are some of the main takeaways for you?

1. **Change your mindset.**

    No matter who we are, our mindset is key to building and maintaining a positive viewpoint of change. If you have a negative mindset, work to change it. I have written about a few ways to create a positive mindset, but there are many more out there.

    Even when you choose to take on a new experience or hobby, you can help to build your positive mental attitude. Every action you take can help you to change your mindset. It is up to you!

2. **Continue to Get Educated**

    When it comes to education, you should never assume that you have learned everything that there is to learn. Part of our growth as individuals is based on our ability to learn from both our experiences, but also those educational opportunities that we seek out on our own. That means no matter what you are willing to try, take the time to learn about it and grow your knowledge and skill set.

3. **Take action**

    No matter what is happening in your world in terms of change, it is important that you do not allow it to paralyze you. Instead, be ready to take action to make that change work for you!

4. **Communicate**

    Throughout this book, I have talked about the importance of education, but also the importance of communication. When you are communicating with your family, friends and professional colleagues, then you are better able to understand them and how change can impact them and your relationships. Remember, too, that communication involves more than talking, but also good listening skills.

These are just a few of the key takeaways from my book on change. Clearly, you need to remember the most important thing is that change happens whether we want it to or not. You need to embrace it for the benefits it can provide in terms of changing your mindset, gaining new skills or even just acknowledging personal growth. The change you see in your lifetime can and likely will have a profound impact. Respect people around you, love your family, embrace your friends, laugh, be happy, and enjoy life. Don't ever be afraid to pursue change and grow with it! To change!!

About the Author

Tony Debogorski is a person committed to personal growth through change. As an author, business entrepreneur, sales management expert and coach, Tony assists others to find their path to the life they want to live. Enhancing the lives of his community, his family and friends, and people around him who wish to find and embrace change.

Tony is married to his lovely wife, Leanne, and has two children. He lives with his family in Canada, while still coaching his hockey team.

Testimonials

"As part of the human condition, we all deal with change. For some of us, it has a greater negative impact than others. Tony's strategies for dealing with change can make anyone change their perspective from change being a negative to a positive!"

Martin Spieker, Trial lawyer, Vancouver

"If you are looking for practical guidance in dealing with life changing events or just the everyday change we encounter, then this is the book. Tony's real life experiences make his strategies come alive in a way that makes them practical and easy to implement."

Mark Grimes, Toronto City Councillor, Toronto

"Life is about constant change. Tony gives you real world strategies to take you from being fearful of change to being excited about the possibilities that change brings. If you want an enjoyable read with practical strategies for your life, then this is that book!"

Bruce Croxon, Entreprenuer, Toronto

"Success takes effort, but on that journey, we all encounter a bump or two that makes us reevaluate where we are headed. Tony's approaches help us to see those bumps as ways to grow instead of obstacles keeping us from moving forward. His book helps you to see change in a different light and I loved it!"

Alex Debogorski, Author, Ice Road Trucker, Yellowknife

"In an era where change is a constant, almost daily occurrence, Tony's strategies and real life experiences are both relatable and practical for individuals at all the points of their life journey. His friendly style and the knowledge that he has been there, done that, makes his tactics even more appealing!"

Mike Schryer, Author – The Facebook Phenomenon, Toronto

"With practical insight, Tony delves into how we make change work for us by sharing tactics that he used throughout his life. His writing grips you, while being relatable. You feel he understands what you are going through, because he has been there! No matter what change you are dealing with, Tony's strategies can work for you!"

Dave Brown, Actor, Xmen, Winnipeg

www.ingramcontent.com/pod-product-compliance
Lightning Source LLC
Chambersburg PA
CBHW070500090426
42735CB00012B/2635